"The reason why *Keeping Ta_* so personal. At no point does Christy Duncan's writing feel white-washed, sanitized, or processed by the usual controls that afflict many spiritual growth books. Rather, what you get is deep, honest introspection and a felt desire to truly help others trapped by a deceitful prison of their own making. The content is relevant, convicting, and God-glorifying. For these reasons I strongly recommend this book!"

—**Dr. Jordan W. Jones,**
Senior Pastor, Belleview Baptist Church,
Burlington, Kentucky; Adjunct Professor of Religion,
Liberty University

"This book is a first-person account of how to overcome your past in hopes of creating a better future. In it, you'll discover what is good and true about the person you are created and called to be."

—**Steve Knox,**
Author of *Confidence: The Science and Art of Self-Belief*

"Christy Duncan's book *Keeping Tally: Illuminating the Lies That Imprison You* is a remarkably candid and transparent telling of her own seduction into depression, anger, and emptiness, a boldly honest confession of her own long, dark journey toward apostasy and sacrilege. Every devoted Christian can relate to her story, identifying the same evil voices that have been harassing us, too. By exposing this poisonous and unrelenting series of demonic lies while demonstrating the nearly tangible power of Scripture and the Holy Spirit, Duncan lays out a trail we can all follow through these dark valleys so we, like herself, can not only quell these demonic attacks, but eventually find ourselves among those captives Jesus led away in his victorious train (Ephesians 4:8). As a pastor, I expect I will be keeping extra copies to give away to my own parishioners who find themselves the target of the Enemy, and who need to rediscover their own place as beloved and redeemed children of God."

—Rev. Ken Southgate,
Pastor, Berea United Methodist Church, Berea, Kentucky

KEEPING TALLY

*Illuminating the Lies
That Imprison You*

Christy Duncan

LUCIDBOOKS

ISBN-10: 1-63296-175-X
ISBN-13: 978-1-63296-175-4
eISBN-10: 1-63296-176-8
eISBN-13: 978-1-63296-176-1

TABLE OF CONTENTS

CHAPTER ONE

A SCHIZOID, A SUICIDAL, AN EXPLOSION, AND A UNICORN

This is not what you're supposed to see
Please, remember me? I am supposed to be
King of a kingdom or swinging on a swing
Something happened to my imagination
This situation's becoming dire
My treehouse is on fire
And for some reason I smell gas on my hands
This is not what I had planned
This is not what I had planned.

—"Forest," Twenty One Pilots

Then he showed me Joshua the high priest standing before the angel of the LORD, and Satan standing at his right hand to accuse him.

—Zechariah 3:1

I've never been hunting, but I have been hunted. At times I fought, at times I ran, and often I built a ridiculous camouflage. I know the enemy's agenda— I've watched him work. He waits until you're weak to make his move. You trip as confusion fogs the truths you once knew. With your sense of direction skewed, he attempts to move closer. If you're too distracted to notice the diversion, you may find yourself walking in his shadow. If you remain there long enough, amnesia grows, and you forget the experience of walking in the light.

How do I know what it feels like to be hunted? Let's start with the climax of the story. I was a pastor's wife ready to leave my faith, my husband, and my three children to move across the country and create a new identity. Running from the pain, I wanted to abandon everything I knew. In my heart, part of me already had.

Wrought with bitterness and consumed with lies, I was a walking, breathing, miserable Christian. Deluded, I believed I was alone. From the smiling faces in church to the happy banter of the Christian radio hosts to the encouraging scriptures posted on social media, all evidence indicated I was the only sheep who had wandered into the hedges. Why was I fighting lies of worthlessness and negative thoughts about my husband while other believers continued on their merry ways? Why couldn't I locate the sin that must be so obvious in my life? Was I the only threat to the enemy that he would choose to corner me? The hopelessness of the lies had brought me to a breaking point, and I could no longer suffer the mental anguish.

Moments before drawing my last breath of faith, a gentle breeze blew, and the dust that had been concealing the truth vanished. This is an account of that story.

* * *

Have you heard the one about the 78-year-old German woman whose home exploded due to a gas leak? She walked out of the house unharmed. It was in the local newspapers. They had a picture of her in front of her home looking like a giant in front of an open doll house. This same lady used to wring chickens' necks with her bare hands. Existing before Bob Barker, she used the heel of her shoe to control the dog and cat populations. Her father took his own life when he was old because he didn't want to be a burden to his family. A lady I know was supposed to deliver a birthday cake to the German lady's home. While she was driving there with the cake, her dog jumped from the back seat onto the cake box and put paw marks on the once beautiful dessert. Terrified, the delivery lady explained what had happened. The old German took her elbow and began putting dents in the rest of the cake, "There," she said. "Now, no one will ever know." That old German was my great grandmother.

At one of the oldest U.S. psychiatric hospitals, there are records of a woman convinced she was being chased by the FBI. She'd make her passengers duck in the back of the car to avoid being seen. She was so convincing that sometimes you started to believe her. When she was on her medications, she was a little less exciting, leaning over in her chair when she passed gas and dreaming she had won bingo in her sleep. She made an incredible

Thanksgiving dinner, and her belly danced when she laughed. I never grew fond of her daytime soaps, but I loved my grandmother nonetheless.

There are many more stories of heritage I could share—shotgun weddings, a few scattered Christians, a child beater, and some alcoholics. The child beater wasn't even one of the alcoholics, just crazy in her own right. One of my grandfathers was convinced I should start growing marijuana. "If we get caught," he said, "you're too young to go to jail, and I'm too old!" He was in the Navy during World War II, but his small lap dog companion made him appear as innocent as a fly. If he were around today, he'd likely be upset that I passed on what could have been a very lucrative business.

Somehow, all these genetics got mixed up in a big pool, and a unicorn was born. Well, at least that's the result you find when you search for scientific answers on the Internet. Apparently, I'm a little bit of an odd breed. Women's minds typically don't function like mine.[1] I'm so odd, in fact, that memes associate finding a woman like me with finding a unicorn. But for the most part, I've mastered the art of appearing normal. I push myself to interact in group settings and try to reveal my true compassion. I attempt to ignore the irritating volume of my surroundings and pretend I'm not afraid that my hooded sweatshirt will strangle me to death. I can achieve the same tasks as everyone else. I've been given enough useful tools to create a pretty good life. The horn and wings only bother me when the elephant costume gets itchy.

When I finished college, I was sure I was on my way to the ultimate quest—the American dream. I had taken the necessary steps, according to the recommendations of society. I graduated from college with honors; married one of those handsome, popular guys; had rich friendships; and pursued ministry opportunities. My husband was a pastor of a church, and I was maintaining the homestead. We were building a pretty little life in the heart of the bluegrass. Before long, I'd be retired, taking cruises, and feeding the neighborhood cats. All was happening according to plan.

But somewhere in the middle of the pursuit, things got hairy. Frustration with my children, my husband, and God felt like a fire I couldn't extinguish. Distorted thoughts kept surfacing, but I couldn't locate the source. I was discontent in every area of my life. I used to be a person in love with God the Creator, but now I didn't care. While skating through my mind, I could tell that things had changed. Ideas that I possessed had been appended. It wasn't enough to make me wipe the hard drive, but I knew things were off. I chose to ignore the questionable and spare the energy of going through an anti-malware scan. I was too tired, too deprived of sleep, too frustrated, too busy to care that the odd invasion was multiplying. I'd think, *Turn on the television and fall asleep. You'll feel better in the morning. It's just some weird phase that will pass, you'll snap out of it.* But it wasn't long before my mind was so disrupted that it felt as though I no longer knew my way around my own house.

It took hindsight to realize what had happened. Amid the hustle and bustle of life, I had been listening to the lies of Satan. My antennas were tuned into his station, and I didn't know when I had changed the channel. As someone who pays attention to detail, I should have recognized his fingerprints and cheap craftsmanship. As a constant observer, I should have known he was there. Although embarrassingly obvious, his ability to prey on our doubts and sinful desires is a prosperous strategy. No matter how much I mocked the naïvety and weakness of Eve (leave the fruit!), I was following right in her footsteps. Millennia later, Satan hasn't changed a bit. Use a tiny element of truth and add a nasty motive for our selfish gain. Use an element of truth and twist it to make you question its validity. Masquerade as an angel of light, and prey on our deceitful hearts. Question what the Lord has told you until Satan gets you to break, enabling him the opportunity to accuse you before the Lord. I left the back gate of my mind open to Satan and his minions. At a time when my flesh was the weakest, I walked straight into the trap.

It's pretty amazing that God doesn't harden his heart toward us. I could have been viewed as a disobedient, self-centered child. I was as ungrateful as they get, believing God had betrayed me. He had plenty of motive to wash his hands of me. Instead, like the prostitute Gomer, the Lord hedged me in. It's what all loving parents do, right? Watch the child throw their nasty fit, making sure their environment is safe, and wait until they are finished with their tantrum in order to speak to them. Even still, God waited to approach me, knowing I couldn't hear him yet for all the distortion in my head. So he sent a band—a band with a sick beat and lyrics you don't hear in churches. I was screaming as loud as I could. But I heard his whisper through these unconventional believers. Although still an ignorant sheep trying to run from the Shepherd, I heard his voice, and it was calling me home.

Once ushered in on the gurney, I experienced quite a series of revelations through the healing process. Most of them are incredibly humbling. There were so many bricks in the wall I had built between myself and the Lord, and most of them were based on childish entitlement. Many came from the heartbreak of viewing situations through the lens of pride. But they were world-approved bricks. They would disguise themselves with clever words, such as, *You have the right to be offended by individuals who have treated you badly.* Not one of the bricks was from an obvious sin that we hear talked about so much that it's like beating a dead horse. I could have been put in the grave at that point, and folks would have gone on and on about how much I loved and served the Lord, but it wasn't true. You don't build a wall between yourself and a person you love. That's not how love works. The Lord's patience and determination to bring me home—that's how love works.

With my stubborn barrier built, I thought I was happy on the other side, alone with no one to frustrate me. But I wasn't alone. I had the company of Satan day and night. It has taken years to air out each lie I believed and sometimes longer to address them. The lies regarding my husband were the most difficult. I've stepped back, sat on the couch, and watched the past 15 years or so of my life through a movie screen. I begin with the odd unicorn attempting to conceal her horn. I watch the film over and over, but I switch hats when doing so. If I view it as the judgmental, perfectionist that I am, I am frustrated at the intensive failures. If I put on the caring, graceful hat, I feel pity for the poor unicorn and want to hold it and nurse it back to health. But when I watch it through the lens of an adversary holding his pitch fork,[2] I am enraged at how this seducer lured a confused, frustrated, lonely unicorn to his van with a few pieces of candy.

Then, right on cue, I see the King rebuke Satan and carry the wounded home. Healed and empowered by her Creator, she's then given a bomb to place in the despicable van. The enemy's plans have been destroyed, and now it's time to drag his tactics into the light.[3]

CHAPTER TWO

THE INVISIBLE PRISON

You grew up true and you grew up right,
But you never saw a day where you had to fight
You need war on your mind.
Cause there's a war, on your mind.

— "War," The Gospel Whiskey Runners

He was a murderer from the beginning, and does not stand in the truth because there is no truth in him. Whenever he speaks a lie, he speaks from his own nature, for he is a liar and the father of lies.

—John 8:44

Have you ever had a friend or acquaintance suggest that you have a certain illness? Just because you have the sniffles and a few hairs fall out, they think you should be seen by a doctor for a life-threatening illness. You may tend to believe that all the thoughts this person offers are bogus and that they watch too many extreme programs on television. Remember when they insisted their invented drink would prolong life by 20 years? Or how they knew the exact day all the stars would fall from the sky? Or when they advised you to hold your infant at 90 degrees with lard on his feet during a full moon for two hours to cure his colic? You trust this person's knowledge as much as the quality of the chalupa you order in a non-Mexican restaurant. Yet later that day, you find yourself Googling their theorized illness, just to be sure. Ah, the power of suggestion.

We humans often think of ourselves as complex and intelligent, immune to subliminal messages, advertising propositions, or scam artist tactics. I'd be one of the first to declare that I've never been fooled by such suggestions, but I prove myself wrong every day. It's not been a lifelong goal of mine to consume a corndog the length of my forearm, but then there's the smell at the fair, and one magically appears in my hand. I make lists for the grocery store in order to stay within budget, but something frivolous always makes its way into the shopping bag. I've reluctantly tried the "desserts" that substitute healthy ingredient options for the indulgent ones, considering the notion that the delicacy will taste just as good. I maintain it's one of the cruelest deceptions one can weave. I will eat a bowl of black beans, and then I will eat my delicious brownie. But I will not be persuaded again into thinking these two things can coexist.

Even the stubborn and the strong-willed have found themselves persuaded. Perhaps we suffer from a touch of overconfidence by believing we are superior to influence. Perhaps, we equally suffer from a bit of foolishness by assuming our ability to be persuaded isn't a major concern. Why should it matter? A subtle suggestion may lead us to cheat on our diet or dodge a chore, but we won't allow ourselves to be influenced on major issues, right? Have you ever encountered a time when you wished you would have stuck to your guns? A time when the situation could have been avoided had you not caved to someone's coaxing? Maybe our tendency to be persuaded is a bigger issue than we think.

What if I told you there's a persuader who has many lifetimes of practice. What if I told you there is a voice that speaks nothing but lies—the master in the art of suggestion, the professional in the field that aims directly for your blind spot? Your best interests are in opposition to his agenda. He has an entourage and masquerades as a beneficial good. He is constantly looking for ways to persuade you. Should we be concerned? Desperately.

Why the dramatic response? Consider his motivation. Why would Satan, the father of lies, desire to persuade us to sin? Because sin equals changing our beliefs about God. And changing our beliefs about God equals an opportunity for the devil to accuse us before the Lord.

Walk with me.

Our very first example in scripture provides perfect insight into the situation. You can only get three chapters into the Bible before humans are deceived. Satan shows up, using the wonderful power of suggestion. What's the result? No biggie, just the fall of man. Please read Genesis 3:1, "Now the serpent was more crafty than any beast of the field which the Lord God had made. And he said to the woman, 'Indeed, has God said?'"

What clever, delicate words, "Indeed, has God said?" We tend to rehearse the theme of this story in our heads as Eve ate the forbidden fruit, disobeying God, and they were kicked out of the garden. We might even think about the consequences of pain in childbirth or in working the land. But what is Satan doing? Was his goal to get Adam and Eve kicked out? Read the phrase again, "Indeed, has God said?" Satan's goal is for Eve to doubt God—His character, wisdom, and love. We often get so caught up with the act of sin that we neglect to examine how our hearts change in order to commit the sin. Here, before Eve ate the fruit, she trusted the Lord. Now, she doubted him. What changed? Sure, an adversary more crafty than any other wild animal had shown up on the scene, but if there's anything I've learned from a few psychology courses, it's that you are in charge of you. Eve gave ear to a lie. She entertained a suggestion. She decided she wanted to be like God— that ultimately worshiping the one true God was not good enough. Eve chose to doubt the Lord, allowing her beliefs about him to change.

For many years I've looked at these types of scripture with the wrong emphasis. How have I missed the heart issue involved? If there's anything Jesus clearly showed us through his time here, it's that God is more concerned about the condition of our hearts than the acts that we perform. The entire Bible is full of stories reflecting this: the widow who gave the smallest coin in circulation, but it was considered more than anyone else had given (Mark 12:42–44); those who thought they were rich and needed nothing and yet the Lord said, "you do not know that you are wretched and miserable and poor and blind and naked" (Rev. 3:17); and the woman who thought touching Jesus's garment would make her well, but it was her faith that healed her (Matt. 9: 20–22). According to 1 Samuel 16:7, "God sees not as man sees, for man looks at the outward appearance, but the LORD looks at the heart."

Although God is faithful to forgive our sins, we are often blind to the full reality of them. I'll put myself out there as an example. If I were to pray for the Lord to forgive me of my sins right now at this moment, it would probably look something like this: "Please forgive me for yelling at my kids, being impatient with my husband, and shooting arrows from my eyes to the lady who tailgated me the entire drive home. Amen."

That's what the folks call "drive-thru ministry." I could at least throw in "please help me to do better the next time." But I often want forgiveness, a clean conscience, and the freedom to go about my day. Who has time to develop more patience?

I assume my shortfalls only affect a few daily operations. Maybe I'll apologize to my children or my husband, but I never consider the condition of my heart or how I've treated the Lord. I don't consider how my actions are reflecting my beliefs about the Almighty God—beliefs painting a portrait that looks nothing like the reflection I thought was in the mirror.

I don't think about the Creator being beside me when I yell in anger at the children he gave as gifts. I don't think about how it implies that his other creations are not as important as I am. When I obviously think it's okay to react out of frustration, I must not believe God was serious about His definition of love. My love appears conditional, and my belief about God's command to love must have changed.

As I criticize my husband through the plank in my own eye, I don't think about the perfect work God is completing in him. I don't think about how I'm placing myself on the judge's seat, implying that the Lord isn't a good enough judge. I neglect the fact that the Lord desires to mold his heart as well. What God may be gently sanding down, I am attempting to rip to shreds. I want a swift sentence and payment, while the Lord desires grace and refinement. I am not trusting the Lord's sovereignty.

And when the lady could have washed the back of my car with her windshield wiper fluid, I don't think of where she may be headed and that the Lord may be in her passenger seat providing comfort as she drives to see her parent for the last time. She has caused me to be flustered, and that is not allowed. She is endangering the well-being of my passengers, so I am justified in shooting arrows of hatred. I have surely assumed that God would be equally upset by this woman's actions, permitting the hatred I am spewing. I have magnified his justice and deleted his grace. I have changed my beliefs about the fullness of God's attributes.

When reflecting on my sin, I rarely consider the Lord, the Creator I claim to love. I apologize for making a mistake, but I never fully realize what I'm doing to his witness. I don't think about the picture I'm painting of him through my unbelief. Neglecting time for reflection and ignoring the Lord through a busy schedule, I allow my heart to become the plant that ceases to produce fruit.

Sin = changing our beliefs about God.

To make our next connection, it will help to have some knowledge of the enemy's camp. Wayne Grudem, a well respected professor of the Bible and theology, defines demons as "evil angels who sinned against God and who now continually work evil in the world."[1] Grudem goes on to list demons' tactics as the use of "lies (John 8:44), deception (Rev. 12:9), murder (Ps. 106:37; John 8:44), and every other kind of destructive activity to attempt to cause people to turn away from God and destroy themselves."[2] In other words, our enemy's end goal isn't to see people sin. It's to see people turn from the Lord.

Even though the enemy may be looking for someone to devour, the funny thing is that his objective has little to do with us. Satan toys around with humans, but his beef is with the Lord. The book of Job serves as a great example of this. Satan was given permission to destroy all of Job's livestock and family and most of his servants and to inflict Job's entire body with painful sores. Satan didn't care about the lives that were lost. He didn't care about the destruction he caused. He wanted Job's heart to change. Satan wanted to show the Lord that Job would "surely curse You to Your face" (Job 1:11). He wanted to see Job turn away from the Lord.

We find another example in the book of Zechariah. Here, the prophet is given a vision: "Then he showed me Joshua the high priest standing before the angel of the Lord, and Satan standing at his right hand to accuse him" (Zech. 3:1). Many scholars believe, based on subsequent verses, that Joshua represents the cleansing of Israel.[3] Joshua is presented wearing filthy garments, and Satan stands ready to condemn. Read the Lord's response, "'The Lord rebuke you, Satan! Indeed, the Lord who has chosen Jerusalem rebuke you! Is this not a brand plucked from the fire?'. . . 'Remove the filthy garments from him.' Again he said to him, 'See, I have taken your iniquity away from you and will clothe you with festal robes'" (Zech. 3:2, 4).

What's the truth about sin? The end goal for Satan is the same for us as it was for Job and for Joshua the high priest—that on that day, Satan could stand before the Lord and accuse us. That Satan could show the Lord that we do not, in fact, love him or believe in him. Satan is solely concerned with his personal vendetta while our eternal lives are at stake.

Sin = changing our beliefs about God = an opportunity to accuse us before the Lord.

We have an adversary, friends. And he is perfectly pleased if all we do is eat a little forbidden fruit, because it means we have chosen to doubt the character of God. Our sins are more than just an act. They reflect the condition of our heart toward God. We can choose to be pawns in Satan's hand or to stand firm in our faith.

Being alert to the ways Satan may be trying to persuade us matters because the result isn't a simple "oopsie." The result is devastating enough that the Son of God was given as a sacrifice. If we are not alert, we could find ourselves manipulated, believing nothing but lies. We may not recognize false teachers. We may fight in every battle except the one that matters—the spiritual war. When we think we are worshiping God, it may be nothing but a golden calf we've created, stripping God of who he is and making him what we want him to be. We could begin to morph the truth of scripture to fit our own agendas, just like Satan did.

* * *

Is it important that we ask the Lord to examine our hearts? That we look deeper than the mistakes we made? That we are transformed by the renewal of our minds? Unless you desire to be manipulated and imprisoned by lies, I urge you to consider some soul-searching while you prepare for battle.

The book of Ephesians describes the armor required for spiritual warfare:

- The breastplate of righteousness
- The shield of faith (to extinguish all the flaming arrows of the evil one)
- The helmet of salvation
- The sword of the Spirit (the word of God)
- Girding your loins with truth
- Shodding your feet with the preparation of the gospel of peace (Eph. 6:14–17)

I'm going out on a limb in supposing that most of us are not in the habit of suiting up for battle every day. Yet many of us could have listed from memory the elements of the armor of God just mentioned. We could also recite this verse without looking it up: "Your adversary, the devil, prowls around like a roaring lion, seeking someone to devour. But resist him, firm in your faith" (1 Pet. 5:8–9).

We have the head knowledge, but we think we never sin. We are lazy and leave off the armor, assuming we will notice Satan when he attempts to tinker in our lives. That's a lot of arrogance or an incredible amount of ignorance. Maybe, it's a whole bunch of both.

* * *

I wish I could say that I had been like Job, maintaining faith in all circumstances. But events transpired, and I set down the shield of faith, exposing myself to lies. While following the Lord, I saw his payment as unjust. The trials were extremely close to proving my faith fraudulent. I was an incredible fool. Jesus had come to set the captives free, but I allowed the lies to hold me in an invisible prison of doubt. The lie that God did not, in fact, want what was best for me formed the foundation. That God was unwilling to step in on my behalf built a ceiling. That God was arrogantly blessing others in spite of me was the wall to which I'd turn my back. He had abandoned me—the barrier that was suffocating. Like Eve, I had allowed myself to be persuaded and to doubt God's character. The lies I believed changed my view of God. The Lord was no longer my friend but rather a foe.

When I could no longer stand the pain of another arrow, I was desperate for healing. It was difficult to find my way back home. How do you find hope in the truth when your walls of imprisonment all scream that the Lord is a liar? I'm here to prove what a faithful God we serve. The Lord slowly started lifting a veil, revealing all the ways I had fallen for the devil's manipulation. I was given a window to see Satan standing outside my prison with his long list of accusations against me. In a scary way, I had been given a glimpse of what it would look like to follow him to the grave. It was much easier than I thought.

Jesus declared that "the gate is wide and the way is broad that leads to destruction, and there are many who enter through it" (Matt. 7:13). The walls began to crumble as I saw Satan for who he really is, and I ran like you wouldn't believe. Literally, I took up running. I was infuriated at what Satan was attempting to do to God's children (including me). I ran to get my emotions out, knowing it's not usually wise to act them out. I ran for clarity, weeding out the lies one at a time. I ran to thank God. Sometimes I ran to remind myself to fight. Often I ran because Satan had a certain lie on replay that day, and I wasn't giving in. I knew I was preparing for battle, but I needed to get my head on straight. I had lost a lot of territory.

The more I ran, the more I desired to cling to the Lord and never let go. I would be his annoying friend, always there, constantly asking what he's up to. I hadn't experienced the intense truth of 1 John 4:19 until I saw what the Lord had saved me from. It reads, "We love, because He first loved us." What depths of despair he has omitted. What filthy garments he has replaced. What love he has shown.

There are many who are going down that wide path, expecting to get a participation ribbon and a happily ever after. But the Lord will spit out those who are lukewarm. And now that I see what heartbreaking accusations were beneath my sins, I can't say I blame him.

I'm certain I'm not the only one who has found themselves spiritually incarcerated. With our deceitful hearts, there are millions of reasons we could end up there. This leads me to the purpose of this book—to crumble the walls of lies I had constructed, chapter by chapter. Why me? Why these specific lies and this book? I have no clue. Perhaps it's because hindsight is 20/20. But I'm sure as heck going to listen to the Lord and his will, praying that if it helps even one of your walls to fall, you will also run out and live in the freedom of the Lord.

Jesus died to set the captives free. It's time to live as free people, slaves only to righteousness.

CHAPTER THREE

YOU DON'T NEED THE CHURCH

If it is not dealt with, offense will
eventually lead to death.
—John Bevere

He died for all, so that they who live might no
longer live for themselves, but for Him who
died and rose again on their behalf.

—2 Corinthians 5:15

L et's talk about what kind of coffee to serve at church. Let's discuss the outreaches, the lighting, the music, enhancing the attractiveness of the stage, deciding where greeters should stand, and what our financial goals are. Let's discuss how to make all generations happy during the service and what type of chairs and carpet we need—or no carpet at all. Let's talk about how to reach the poor and the rich and seem edgy and cool but never upset anyone with the truth of the gospel. Let's figure out how we can double our numbers.

Or let's not, because I'm really tired of being part of these discussions. I understand that there may need to be organization around topics to maintain order, but the business side of the church makes my stomach turn a little. Too much man-made effort makes the whole thing seem off when God is supposed to be involved. I get confused and forget whether we need to be focusing on the people attending or the God we are worshiping. Either way, the logistics of the church are not the real problem. People are what's wrong with the church, right? You finally get your friend to come along with you and they are hurt by some ignorant comment made by John Doe following the service. Your other friend won't come at all because they insist everyone there is a hypocrite. You have even spilled the beans a few times to these friends about the gossip and your own distrust. The church is full of broken people, often acting like they have it all together. Who needs more of that in their lives?

I'm not special. All of these issues have bothered me at one time or another. However, none of them are the real problem. They are not what is keeping you from desiring to be part of the church. You're barking up the wrong tree, my friend.

* * *

Forgive me for sharing another quote from Wayne Grudem, but his words cut me so deeply, they must be shared. He goes into detail with examples from scripture, but here is a glimpse of his thoughts about how to recognize demonic influence: "In severe cases of demonic influence, as reported in the Gospels, the affected person would exhibit bizarre and often violent actions, especially opposition to the preaching of the gospel."[1]

The quote sounds horrific and impossible for a believer, but when I first read it, I immediately knew, "Yep, that's me." I wasn't busting out of chains every day or cursing Jesus to his face, but I was a modern more sedated version of it. I initially told my husband that the violent actions didn't pertain to me. He told me I was wrong. When it comes to fight or flight, I soar like an eagle. I wanted to abandon my family. That may be one of the most violent acts a person can perform. My husband was right. But the even harder slap on the face was realizing that all of my actions revealed an "opposition to the preaching of the gospel." And where did I construct the walls that led me there? Right in the middle of the church.

So what's my church sob story? Have you ever been left to care for seven to ten young, diaper-wearing children by yourself for at least two hours during what's supposed to be their naptime? You look like a tornado blew through you at the end when someone asks, "How'd it go?" And there was so much, so fast. You can't describe why your eye is twitching or whose stool is on your elbow, or that at one point you thought they may all die, but they now appear just fine. That's how my story goes. It was a lot, from all angles, all at once—from three family members passing away, to children with broken bones, to emptying all our savings and retirement. We were called by the Lord to join other believers in planting a new church. My husband had been invited to participate as a co-planter and associate pastor. We put it all on the line. It was a 24/7 roller coaster of exhaustion, excitement, mystery, and mourning, but we were thrilled to be part of the ride.

We were young and willing to serve, seeking elders to disciple, nurture, and encourage us. Although not typically described as vulnerable, we happily made ourselves that way for father figures (those the Lord appointed over us) in the church. We trusted without reservation and pursued the Lord at the speed of light. The church plant had been formed on biblical doctrine and agreed upon by what was then declared the elders, a noble group of men (my husband being one of them). The church body grew rapidly in numbers, but we soon began scratching our heads as we sat listening to the teaching of a differing, illegitimate doctrine—one man's dogma. The group of elders were then declared board members, which in this context had the intended effect of creating yes men. One by one, the leader shifted things until they no longer coincided with our discerning spirits. The truth of scripture was being disregarded in the preaching. My husband and I watched with sorrow as the Lord began releasing from this church those who could rightly divide scripture, those who had become as precious as blood relatives to us. And then our turn came. Like a marriage that is ripped apart, we mourned desperately what was lost. What had been put on the line disappeared, and we were left with nothing.

So what's so ironic about our story? Apparently, this story has been around for decades. When you pick up a book today and find that the author essentially penned your same story nearly 20 years earlier, you freeze in place. That happened to me, and I want to share a bit of this fella's work for two reasons: (1) It is nearly guaranteed that someone reading this has had a similar story, and (2) the healing we found from this man's words was the Lord's cure for our struggling souls.

In John Bevere's book *The Bait of Satan: Living Free from the Deadly Trap of Offense*, he lays on the table the fact that we will be hurt in this life. Whether we choose to be offended by a person or to forgive is where our root of bitterness either flourishes or ceases to exist. He hit my personal nail on the head when he devoted a chapter to being offended by church fathers:

> Many leaders in our homes, corporations, and churches are more concerned with their goals than with their offspring. Because of this attitude, these leaders view God's people as resources to serve their vision instead of seeing the vision as the vehicle to serve the people. The success of the vision justifies the cost of wounded lives and shattered people. Justice, mercy, integrity, and love are compromised for success. Decisions

are based on money, numbers, and results. . . . How many leaders have cut off men under them because of suspicion? Why are those leaders suspicious? Because they are not serving God. They are serving a vision.[2]

Bevere compares these situations to how Saul treated David. If you remember, David was given into Saul's care by the Lord. Then Saul continued to relentlessly pursue the death of David without cause. Bevere states, "This was a prime opportunity for David to be offended—not only with Saul but also with God."[3]

This was the beginning of the climax of my story. This is where I exchanged the shield of faith for Satan's bait. Let me declare here that Satan's tactic is stinking sneaky. Whether or not my perception of those years in ministry was 100 percent factual, I had felt betrayed and cut to the core. What I didn't realize was the choice I was making in response. In silence, I chose to be bitter toward a man, then toward those who supported that man, and then toward the Lord for allowing the situation to occur. Justification for my feelings plowed the fields, and seeds of bitterness grew like an invasive species.

But here's the thing about bitterness: once planted, it seems to grow whether or not you are actively feeding it—like when you find an old bag of garden bulbs in the basement that have long sprouts. In truth, my husband and I thought we had moved past these issues. We thought we had forgiven our brothers in the church and taken our share of the blame. My husband had sought reconciliation, and I tried to rejoice in the good that continued to occur in that body of believers. What I didn't notice was my persistent reaction to the Lord. I was hurt and had chosen my typical inclination of taking flight. I thought I'd just soar for a while until the pain stopped, until I was done being angry with the Lord. I'd enter back into communion with him once he restored the garden I was supposed to be living in. Joy was the direct opposite of my reaction to this trial, and the Lord seemed unwilling to right what had been wronged.

* * *

Hatred crept in slowly. Okay, I'll go back to Christian music. There's very little of it that I actually care for. There, I said it. Something in me changed while I was pouting, though. I used to dislike the lack of creativity in the music itself, but then I began to despise the lyrics too. In the beginning, I assumed it was because I had always been annoyed with the repetitiveness. I know that words are repeated for emphasis, but if I repeat something, I want to mean what I say each time, and I'm usually out of authenticity by round three. The lyrics were so innocent and shallow. How can a depressed or hurting person identify with song lyrics that do not mention these emotions? All of it seemed so saturated with an effort to be both trendy and mainstream while the actual words felt like an advertisement. What was supposed to be as intimate as sex in marriage was just another cheesy, money-making performance. As soon as I got in the car, I'd switch the Christian channel my husband had set on the radio.

I had the same hardened heart toward Christian talk radio. Although I respected many of the early morning pastors, by the time I had to run errands in the afternoon, less appealing folks were on air. More infomercials. I'd pop in CDs.

In an effort to survive my battle wounds, I became even more of a hermit. I didn't feel as though I could share the pain with others because it seemed impossible to do so without tearing down God's people. I only had a handful of very close friends, but I didn't expose my feelings to them either. I'd talk with my husband, but a wounded soldier can only do so much for another wounded soldier. For many months, we wandered throughout the house, my face reflecting anger, his confusion. My husband was willing to wait for the explanations he sought and continue in pursuit of the Lord. In contrast, I turned my back on God, demanding justice. My unwillingness to forgive birthed a divide in our marriage. And in the end, I was like Job's wife, wondering why my husband wouldn't just let go of his integrity and blame God.

By this time, we were at another church—our current church. The people were genuine, but the effort to conduct a church service felt like pulling teeth. It seemed like most of the individuals involved were overwhelmed by responsibilities outside the church. The majority of the tasks fell back on my husband and our family. We stored the sound equipment in our already cramped house. My husband spent half his free time away from me and the kids, setting up for the service, singing, teaching, tearing down after the service, and attending leadership meetings. It felt so much like work—I despised all of it. I had become resentful toward the entire Sunday morning "process." You did not want me as a volunteer since my heart was light years away from doing anything for God's glory. I could care less if I were to miss one, two, or the entire next year's services. In fact, doing so would have brought a smile to my face.

I was still flapping away, not speaking to the Lord because I was done listening to his silence. I eventually stopped picking up the Bible because I couldn't find anything new, nothing that was helping the situation. Somehow, whenever I read the verses, I kept hearing them in a generic show announcer's voice. The words that used to be alive now flew right into the Christianese box. I couldn't separate the human teachers I had heard using them from the God who had written them.

And books on Christian spirituality? Ha! I would run as far from that side of the bookstore as possible.

Sum it all up and you get a gal with a hardened heart who has just about cut off every typical way people expect to hear from the Lord. I thought it was all just a matter of preference. I didn't like everything that other believers were doing. I thought my anger was because of the cookie-cutter Christians I kept running into. But there was a common thread among the things that repulsed me. It wasn't that they were too worldly or that they were unjust. It wasn't that they abused people or that there were false teachers. It wasn't the music or the lighting. It wasn't the structure of the service or the people involved. The common thread was the preaching of the gospel. I had walked away from the mirror for so long that I had no idea what I had become.

If you had asked me at the time if I were opposed to the preaching of the Word, I would have said no. But sometimes, actions speak louder than words. I was a tree loaded with apples who claimed that it was not, in fact, an apple tree. It took five years for me to move from a light on a hill to a boarded-up, abandoned shack. How can a person end up like this, someone who has stumbled along behind Jesus for 20 years? Elementary, my dear Watson, elementary.

How to Get Someone out of Church 101

- Omit Ephesians 6:12.
- Let people do what comes naturally: Hurt one another.
- Encourage them that they have the right to be offended.
- Help them attach all of that pain to God and the gospel.
- Let them leave the people and the Word while maintaining what they call a "relationship" with God.

It's pretty simple. It worked for me—hook, line, and sinker.

* * *

So, why are so many folks choosing to abandon the church (whether physically or metaphorically)? I submit to you the book of Ephesians, chapter 6, verse 12: "For our struggle is not against flesh and blood, but against the rulers, against the powers, against the world forces of this darkness, against the spiritual forces of wickedness in the heavenly places." Our battle is a spiritual one to defend the truths of the gospel against lies, but we are off slaying our own flesh and blood. We are distracted with what we can see instead of what is unseen. We are being deceived.

I'm convinced that Bevere's book *The Bait of Satan* isn't more popular in Christian circles because its truth is such a hard pill to swallow. Even though we will be wronged in this life, there are many verses of scripture to encourage us, as Jesus did, to choose to not be offended by others. Bevere wrote, "Just because you were mistreated, you do not have permission to hold on to an offense."[4] How many people did I lose just now? It's tough, right? That pride and animalistic desire to defend yourself swells up as soon as you read the statement. Being hurt by those you love and trust can fill in the blanks as some of the worst days you have experienced. But the opposite of being offended is forgiveness, and how many times does Scripture tell us to forgive?

I wish I could quote Bevere's entire book, but I'll use self-restraint and offer only one more sentence: "Offense is a tool of the devil to bring people into captivity."[5] Boom! There you have it. That was the sin that opened the door for the construction of my prison of lies. I chose to be offended by members of the body of Christ. I believed that my battle was with them. At the least, I was distracted enough with the frustration to forget about the real enemy and put down the armor. It led to bitterness and a hardened heart toward the church, the Word, and the Lord. It nearly led to my own destruction.

So many of us are falling for Satan's lies. We refuse to forgive others because we determine that forgiveness is impossible (try Jesus's explanation in Matthew 18: 21–35). We love conditionally, the opposite of God's love (how about the entire book of Hosea). We treat others as they deserve, withholding grace (Romans 5:8: "But God demonstrates His own love toward us, in that while we were yet sinners, Christ died for us"). Altogether, it's quite a nasty picture of community, but we keep falling for it. We refuse to let go of the pain someone caused us. We refuse to address others we have wronged. We bicker and battle among one another. We look like a building full of crooked politicians, a smile on our faces with resentment, hatred, distrust, and judgment seeping through our teeth.

Conversely, could you imagine being in a group of people who love others as they love themselves, are quick to forgive one another, and keep no record of wrongs committed? It would almost be as though those people were acting like Jesus. When a person makes a mistake, they are approached in private, out of love, and given many opportunities for repentance. Reconciliation would most often occur. They'd exhibit the most beautiful human relationships people had ever seen. Everyone would want to know why they were so different. Many would want to be part of that community. It would be as though they were tapped into living water that flowed throughout each one of them. It would look like what teachers speak of in the Bible. What a beautiful idea scripture paints—an image as beautiful as a bride on her wedding day.

* * *

What does this lie—You don't need the church—claim?

It claims that you are what's most important. Your contentment is the greater good. You shouldn't have to submit yourself to spiritual authority. Life should serve you instead of you serving others. It claims that God did not know what he was doing when he formed the body of Christ and when he established the church. It claims that all those letters written to churches by the apostles weren't written to refine the church, just to refine you. It claims that God is a liar. It claims that Jesus didn't die for his bride but only for you.

It's not safe for a sheep to be out wandering on its own. Trust me, I've tried it.

* * *

It's such a strange feeling to be thankful to the Lord for revealing my faults. I was overcome with relief when he showed me the rocks I had used in constructing my heart of stone. I never thought of myself as super prideful, but feeling as though I was justified in my bitterness was a sneaky arrogance I hadn't caught. Holding on to offense truly can bring death. Give it a few years, and you might eventually be opposed to the preaching of the Word as well. Releasing the people you feel have wronged you has a more positive effect on your own being than anything else, more relief than anyone can describe. You will just have to experience it for yourself.

CHAPTER FOUR

YOU'RE WORTHLESS

You are my Lord; I have no good besides You.

—Psalm 16:2

When I was about eight years old, my parents pressured me to enter the greased pig contest at the county fair. If you've never heard of a greased pig contest or if you are not from Kentucky, here's the gist. Some folks get a big hog and cover it in Crisco. All the children wait in the arena for the signal. The pig is released, the alarm is sounded, and whoever pins the pig to the ground first wins the money. Along with me, there were about 20 other kids who were pressured by their parents to be the butt of this joke. But I had a genius brother who said, "See how the whole group runs in the same direction? The pig darts out to the other side and no one is over there to get him. Stay on the opposite side, wait until he runs out from the group and grab him!"

I got the pig. I think it's the squealing that usually freaks people out and makes them release the slippery swine. Competitive people will agree to do some ludicrous stuff just because they enjoy winning. The news interview following the event is currently my only claim to 15 seconds of fame.

A couple of years later, I went with my parents to an outdoor outlet mall. My dad and I tire quickly, so we sat in a lobby full of flies for an hour. Being the well-rounded father that he is, he taught me how to catch a fly with my bare hand. Very, very slowly you set your slightly opened hand about four inches behind the fly. Then, with tenacious speed, you sweep your hand toward the fly, closing your fingers. From there, you have two choices: squeeze your fist tightly, squishing the pest to its death, or slam the nuisance as hard as you can to the floor, keeping your foot ready to end whatever is left of him. I prefer the second method, even when I occasionally look like a fool, unknowingly missing the fly and throwing a handful of empty air to the ground with all my might.

Most people would agree that it would be ridiculous for me to gain my self-worth from the fact that I am a greased-pig-contest-winning flycatcher. I probably wouldn't go very far in a talent show. I'm batting a thousand in the swine-catching arena. But what if I miss the next one? Then I'm just the gross girl who catches flies. I'm not sure these traits are the best ones to choose in establishing my value. Maybe if I added the fact that I've high-fived Batman? But it was the least favorite version of all the Batman films and probably not worth mentioning.[1]

So many of us are constantly searching for evidence supporting our value as a person. We naïvely fight against Satan's accusation of inadequacy. Sometimes, we are well aware of his presence, tormented by his lies of how we don't measure up. Sometimes, we live years smiling at him as he tells us how great we are, comparing ourselves to those around us. We are hearing his lies and choosing to try to defend ourselves to him. In the process, we are wasting our opportunity to be ambassadors for Christ.

In some form or fashion, we each hear the lie that we are worthless. From there, we are split into three groups: those who believe the lie, those who use the world's scorecard to combat the lie, and those who live for the Lord.

* * *

My People

I'm not exactly the most compassionate person on the planet. My parents held their breath as I became a mom for the first time. There really is something to be said about natural instincts. Motherhood aside, there is another group of people for which I have deep compassion. I can usually spot them across a crowded room. Their presence, although non-intrusive, is known to me. It's not so much the type of clothes they wear or their hairstyle. It's not how antisocial or awkward they appear. It's the sadness in their eyes and the old soul behind them that begs to be set free. It's the heightened awareness that they are in this world but not of it. It's the face of a person who hears the lies distinctly and is weary from the battle. It's the same face I see when I look in the mirror.

But what I know about these people is not always congruent with what I determine about myself. They are humble and teachable. Compassion and understanding flow endlessly out of them. They value integrity and authenticity, and they represent ideals. They are some of the most unnoticed, beautiful people in the world. But often, they want to die. They want the pain to stop. They are tired of feeling worthless. Weary from the fight, they have succumbed to the lie. And my eyes fill with tears because I know I see them as God does, and it's his Spirit within me that is mourning.

As I said before, our enemy has no moral code. He has no problem telling us we are worthless, especially if it keeps us focused on ourselves, turning our minds from the Lord. Sometimes, it's his favorite scab to scrape away, knowing that someone else inflicted the wound long ago and that there is little he must do to remind us of our worthlessness. Satan will likely try to keep us in the perfect balance, just enough pain and self-doubt to pause our relationship with the Lord, distracted again by believing we are unworthy but never in enough pain to send us running to God. Satan is attempting to murder God's people emotionally while his goal is to accuse them of never believing Jesus. For if we don't believe we have value, how can we believe we have been made righteous? What do our actions reveal about our faith? Do they not reflect the belief that we will never measure up, as though we are holding ourselves to the old law and as if Christ had not come?

This isn't a topic I speak of lightly. While growing up, I knew there would always be someone smarter, prettier, or more athletic, so I didn't attempt to use my accomplishments as a basis for self-worth. I tried to appreciate the traits the Lord had given me as his creation, but as a young person, it was difficult to hold on to a small whisper when confronting the contradicting message of a boisterous world. In case you don't know, unicorns experience the awkward stage as much as everyone else when becoming an adult. My vice was to hitch my wagon to a man for worth. Like a dog returns to its vomit, this fool continued in her folly. I would remove the robe of righteousness in exchange for filthy rags. I reflected the image of a broken cistern, not the image of Christ.

Needless to say, I understand this group of tormented people. Like a mother hen, I wish I could gather this flock and run them to safety. I wasted years of my life believing this lie until I fully submitted myself to the Lord for his healing. In secret, I daily sought him. In full honesty, I shared my anger, pain, sorrow, and doubt. Much of the healing came when I let go. These lies become your parasitic friends. Strangely, you have to be willing to let them die. The beautiful thing about finding healing in the Lord is that you don't develop a false sense of pride and worth. Your value is established and magnified and cannot be stripped from you. Authentic, true healing can only be found in the Creator. And then you will know what David was talking about when he said of the Lord, "He restores my soul" (Ps. 23:3).

If we are "ambassadors for Christ, as though God were making an appeal through us" (2 Cor. 5:20), how will the world hear the appeal through our voice of self-hatred? We must allow the truth to point us to Christ, to stop being consumed with thoughts about ourselves, and to start being the ambassadors we are called to be. With whatever energy we have and whatever time we are given, we must seek the Physician and ask for healing.

Of course, the truth is that we are so valuable to the Lord that Christ died for us. We are children of the King, shielded by his power through our faith, but we must have faith.

The Gladiators

So maybe you're ready to skip this chapter because self-worth isn't a struggle for you, or at least it hasn't been since you were a wee babe. Let's just double check really quickly to make sure we haven't missed any subtle lies along the way.

Look at these situations and ask yourself if your value as a person would change if any of them occurred: you begin to lose your hair; the promotion was given to someone else; your all-star kid is now in his 30s and lives in your basement; you earn half the paycheck of your friends; your car's window is replaced with a trash bag and tape. Would you still walk with the same posture? Would you worry about other people's opinions of you? Are you worried they might eventually adopt the same disparaging thoughts about you that you have of yourself? Would your sense of value change because of your circumstances?

What about in these contexts: your parents are wealthy; you finish at the top of your private school; you have hundreds of followers on social media; you are a doctor in your field of study and your paycheck reflects it; you can send your children to the most renowned camps in the country; you are the leader of several volunteer organizations. Would you walk tall? Are you now valuable because of your status?

Without honest self-reflection, each of us can fall prey to looking to the world's opinion for our worth. Like gladiators, we tear each other down and compare ourselves to each other. Jealousy creeps in, and we become consumed with selfish ambition. Pride seeps into our hearts because we've credited the good we have received to our own efforts instead of to the Lord. What we have or have achieved is for us and thanks to us. We have adopted the world's wisdom because we believe the proud should inherit the earth.

Remember the words used by James?

Who is wise and understanding among you? By his good conduct let him show his works in the meekness of wisdom. But if you have bitter jealousy and selfish ambition in your hearts, do not boast and be false to the truth. This is not the wisdom that comes down from above, but is earthly, unspiritual, demonic. For where jealousy and selfish ambition exist, there will be disorder and every vile practice. But the wisdom from above is first pure, then peaceable, gentle, open to reason, full of mercy and good fruits, impartial and sincere. And a harvest of righteousness is sown in peace by those who make peace.

—James 3:13–18 ESV

And do you remember the words of Paul? "For who regards you as superior? What do you have that you did not receive? And if you did receive it, why do you boast as if you had not received it" (1 Cor. 4:7)?

We cannot be distracted from our purpose: "Let your light shine before men in such a way that they may see your good works, and glorify your Father who is in heaven" (Matt. 5:16). Everything about us should point to the Lord, causing others to glorify him. If we are seeking our own glory and justification, are we not like the salt that has become tasteless?

What does the lie "you're worthless" attempt to distract us from? It distracts us from our purpose to be ambassadors for Christ. We become consumed with the need to validate ourselves to Satan, replacing God's will with his, replacing God's glory for our own.

The Meek

There are those who believe the Lord. They believe, in humility, that they were created in the image of God. They believe that in his loving kindness, God sent his son as a ransom for the ungodly. They believe that they are new creations, being justified through Christ. They believe they are given value through the Lord. They are filled with gratitude and praise. They "no longer live for themselves, but for Him who died and rose again on their behalf" (2 Cor. 5:15).

If you believe the truth of the gospel, you must believe you have worth. If you believe you have worth, you must live your life for the one from whom your worth first came.

CHAPTER FIVE

YOU MUST CONFORM

Indeed the safest road to Hell is the gradual one—the gentle slope, soft underfoot, without sudden turnings, without milestones, without signposts.

—C.S. Lewis

For better or worse, my aunt was a person you typically wouldn't forget once you were introduced to her. Okay, truthfully, you might remember her even without a formal introduction. She was the only banana in the football stands suited up head to toe in yellow rain gear at the first sight of any passing cloud. She was the only adult who wore the plastic bibs provided for kids in restaurants. She was the only one I knew who continued to raise the roof wherever she went, well into the twenty-first century. She was quirky, and like all of us, she had some traits that rubbed people the wrong way. But she was never bothered by the impressions she made, and there's something to be said for that. For years, she demanded that I raise the roof at her funeral when they carried her casket past, knowing she would be going home to Jesus. I knew I should honor her request, but I would have been perceived as an insensitive fool. Instead, during my portion of the eulogy, I led the crowd in raising the roof for her. It was incredible to watch all those well-dressed folks sitting in a beautiful church, raising the roof. It was difficult to maintain my composure as I pictured my aunt happily laughing at the sight. I like to think it's the only time it's been done at a funeral. It was different, like her.

Speaking of unusual people, let me throw this at you. I am an insane, stay-in-the-line rule-follower, but I hate being told to conform. It seems contradictory, right? By following rules, you are conforming. But consider the dynamics of a basketball game. All the team members play by the same rules, but they all behave quite differently from each another. None of them are allowed to walk with the ball, but only half of them have the ability to dunk. None of them are permitted to double dribble, but only a few have the ball handling skills required to quickly bring it down the court. What if the coaches told the point guards (those are the main ball-handling ones) to become centers (those are the massive dudes under the basket)? They'd be setting picks every other step and attempting to dunk from the three-point line. And let's be honest, they'd probably be slower than all the other teams. I don't think they'd end up winning the game. It's good to be well-rounded, but all the players have specific talents that make them perfect for the positions they fill. They comply with the rules, but they are different. They are disciplined, but they do not all conform the same.

The basketball example is a pleasant thought because it's a scenario where differences are celebrated. But does that mean it's easy to be different in other spheres of life? Do we typically celebrate our intrinsic differences, or do we conform to a standard? If you got the itch to start dancing, would you break it down in a mall? Would you wear white pants in January? If the joy you had was inexplicable, would you sing as you walked alone through the park? Would you ride a grocery cart 20 yards to your car because the parking lot is perfectly sloped and the efficiency of doing so is off the charts?

My daughter painted a picture that hangs on the desk where I write. It's the face of a lion and his robust mane. She chose to fill the mane with fiery red, yellow, and orange. She did the same for the caption, which reads, "Creativity takes Courage."

Why does the caption make sense? Why does it resonate with people? Because it's safe to move with the flow of traffic and time-saving to agree. It's comforting to be a horse in a field of horses. It's enjoyable because you're surrounded by others who are like you, and there is little risk. But creativity—difference—takes courage.

Sometimes, attempting to conform to the norm can be excruciating. Lefties know what I'm talking about, right? How many times have they been dismayed due to the inconvenience of their handedness? The south paws must live in a right-handed world with all of its frustrations. They are constantly aware of the fact that they are different and that their difference is inconvenient, if to no one else but themselves. Nevertheless, it's never fun to feel like an inconvenience.

When you are part of the majority, you don't often think about these folks. You don't consider the frustrations of the food allergy sufferer or the color-blind. You don't think about a building's accessibility to wheelchairs or that some people can't reach items on the top shelves. The general population is not choosing to be insensitive. They just find it much simpler to go with the majority.

But the truth is that many people are hurting because they are different. They don't need to be teased or left out of activities to feel pain. Sometimes the repetitive, subtle message to become like everyone else is enough to cause sorrow. It's sorrowful because it's a message communicating that when the Creator made them, he messed up. I know, because I am one of those people.

Some may think it's boastful to talk about my unicorn-like personality, but they would be wrong. According to certain statistics, you'll only find four women out of 500 who interact with the world the way I do.[1] That's the same as eight out of 1,000, the same as 16 out of 2,000. I know, you're impressed with my math skills, but let's look at the incredible loneliness these statistics can represent. Imagine being put in a group for a project and how often you'd get a like-minded teammate. Remember the comfort of being a horse in a field of horses? Others may not notice the horn on my head, but I am always aware of its presence.

I try to smile at the unusual way my mind thinks, continuing to ride the grocery cart to the car and making jokes when I probably shouldn't. I remind myself that I'm still a female even though I hate pink and cheerleading and most romantic comedies. If I want to act like I'm pole vaulting while using the umbrella to dodge a giant puddle, I do so. I don't mind a few quizzical looks. But every once in a while, when I perceive expressions of criticism, I'll pour a bucket of water on the fire within. I'll try to act like everyone else. I'll conform.

I'm not sure the content of this chapter will resonate with the majority. But perhaps it needs to be considered by everyone so they know how to respond to their unique brothers or sisters in Christ. Are the odd balls welcomed in churches, or do they mostly find themselves interacting with groups outside the church? If they find themselves more comfortable outside the church, is it the truth of the gospel that offended them or the judgmental looks of disapproval? Maybe we are unintentionally assuming that God's creativity in some people is too risky. Maybe we should do a gut check of our control issues. Either way, if we are not careful, the message to conform can be a deadly poison.

* * *

Let's end any speculations before they begin. The Bible calls sin lawlessness (1 John 3:4). The Bible describes sin in such depth that it even includes sins of omission and sins of the heart. Consider Matthew 5:28, which says, "But I say to you that everyone who looks at a woman with lust for her has already committed adultery with her in his heart." God has blessed us with the standards for living a holy life for our own benefit, encouraging growth in our spiritual lives. We believe in adhering to those standards because we trust the wisdom of God. We submit ourselves to God because we believe he is who he claims to be. We have criteria to live by and rejoice in the Lord's transforming of our minds to be like his.

At no time do I want this chapter to suggest that I am saying we should not obey the Lord's commands. The Lord's appeal for us to be imitators of him is out of love for us and for his glory.

Satan's message of conformity is different.

* * *

I remember leaving church filled with anger, hurt, and confusion. I was growing weary from the condemnation that whispered,

> *The type of person you were created to be is wrong. God is displeased with his design. You need to conform to the persona of the masses. You need to smile when you don't feel like it. You need to be outgoing. You need to stop thinking so much and talk more with other people. Forget the ways you*

think the Lord might be using someone like you, and
follow this man-made road to righteousness.

I was confused because the anger I felt was brought on by a sermon, a sermon I kept hearing again and again. It was a sermon that left other people smiling. They seemed to love these types of talks. They seemed to thrive on them. Why did I feel so different?

You will have to show me grace as I work through this on paper. My ideas on the matter may not be very popular.

I was angry because I continued to hear a message from the stage telling me to be more extroverted. The only ways I could serve as the gospel commanded was through the church's outgoing outreach activities. I had never felt the Lord press upon my heart to hand out a turkey to a stranger and then conjure up a conversation, but that's what I was being asked to do. It wasn't that I didn't want to feed the hungry, as Jesus commanded. It wasn't that I didn't want to spread the gospel out of love for Jesus. I wanted to be disciplined in all areas scripture calls us to be. I didn't want to hand out a turkey with an uncomfortable smile on my face and pretend I had an instant connection with a stranger, because the acts were as unauthentic to a person like me as they get. They felt unauthentic because I didn't know the person. I could serve out of the love I had been shown by God, but without God's blessing of empathy for these people already established in my heart, I knew they'd see right through me. Yet I felt condemned for not conforming to the exact mode of service the sermon had decreed. Sermon after sermon that said "Be uncomfortable by talking excitedly to hundreds of strangers" brought tears to my eyes. It felt like a message proclaiming that God would never be pleased with me unless I became an extroverted, happy-go-lucky, corny-joke-telling Christian. (Okay, I added the corny-joke telling part). Denying myself in order to follow Christ seemed to not only mean I must die to my flesh but also that the design the Lord used in creating me must die with it. I must conform to today's version of what a die-hard Christian looks like—the always-happy-to-see-you, event-loving Christian.

Ironically, I don't mind talking to strangers. In stores or at the park I'm comfortable having conversations with people next to me, and I'm genuinely happy, smiling, and cracking jokes while doing so. I don't go out specifically to find someone to witness to, but I'm open to sharing the gospel message if God asks me to. It's my earnest intent to always be living out the gospel, whether I speak of it or not. I want to display God's character wherever I am. For nearly all the strangers I've met, I'd happily give them a free turkey. I enjoy meeting new people and having the chance to indirectly or directly share the love of Christ. So it begs the question, what in the world was my issue with the sermons?

First, I'd like to note the difference between being disciplined and conformity. When referring to a person who is disciplined, you are referring to someone who adheres to rules of conduct.[2] So a disciplined follower of Jesus would be someone who adheres to living out the commands and commissions given in scripture.

Conformity refers to people adapting to or being accommodating toward the standards of society.[3] It looks like a masquerade, the outward acts not reflecting what is inside the person.[4] So a follower of Jesus might be conforming to the world today by engaging in premarital sex. Their beliefs regarding Jesus are held internally, while their outward expressions do not reflect their beliefs.

From these descriptions, maybe it's easier to tell why I was bothered. The messages, through my ears, were not encouraging me to be disciplined in the commands of scripture—to serve, to love, to show forgiveness—because of Jesus and for Jesus. The messages were telling me to change who God created me to be from an introverted, deep thinking, genuine person to an extroverted, insanely happy person, because that is what constitutes effective service in one person's opinion.

You'll likely know these verses:

> Therefore I urge you, brethren, by the mercies of God, to present your bodies a living and holy sacrifice, acceptable to God, which is your spiritual service of worship. And do not be conformed to this world, but be transformed by the renewing of your mind, so that you may prove what the will of God is, that which is good and acceptable and perfect.
> —Romans 12:1–2

What exactly does the apostle Paul mean by not conforming to "this world"? John MacArthur, a respected pastor and author, describes "this world" in this verse as "the system of beliefs, values—or the spirit of the age—at any time current in the world. This sum of contemporary thinking and values forms the moral atmosphere of our world and is always dominated by Satan (cf. 2 Cor. 4:4)."[5]

I'll pose my very delicate question now. Is it possible that the values and beliefs of the world today—the spirit of the age—could be one whose front is service to the poor, abused, and neglected of society? Is it possible that Satan could desire the moral atmosphere to mimic the true callings of Christians? If this could be true, how could those in the world tell the difference between Christians who serve and any other civic organization?

All the knee-jerk reactions said this: Because we serve out of love for Jesus. I desperately hope this is the case because if it's possible for Satan to enhance acts of service through the spirit of the age, we'd better make sure we, as the church, are doing what we do because of the gospel, informed at each turn by the gospel, and for the glory of God. Otherwise, what we are doing is fruitless. We need to make sure that we are doing an act of service because the Lord has commissioned us to do so, not because it's the new, trendy, social justice thing to be involved in. With such a fine line, we must be devoted to the transforming of our minds so we are not simply conforming to this world and thus dropping our witness to Jesus.

* * *

I heard a radio host break down on air the other day. I think it's the first time I've ever heard this happen. A child, thousands of miles away from the radio host's home, had been taken from its parents because the parents had low IQs. When the radio station interviewed the mother, no one would have guessed she wasn't "normal." When the social worker arrived at the home, the child was not in any danger. The radio host broke down and struggled through the story because his daughter has cerebral palsy. Overcome with empathy, he couldn't continue his sentences without long pauses to regain his composure. He couldn't help imagining his daughter, the most caring, nurturing, loving person he knew, having her child taken from her. I can't see how anyone listening to this radio host could have held back their tears. This God-fearing man was truly moved by compassion to help these parents get their child back. His compassion and true empathy made me want to join the cause.

Why did the turkey sermon bother me? Truthfully, because it felt like a pep rally. It felt like a pep rally because it was a shallow sermon based on service with an itty, bitty tagline about Jesus. If we could lure people from the other side of the tracks with a turkey, maybe they'd see how hip, cool, and friendly we are and want to come to our church. It felt like the underlying message was to invite people to church to boost the numbers, not to make true disciples. I wondered why we needed all the hype and energy from the stage to go do these acts of service. I guess we needed the hype and guidance because we are lazy, right? Are we lazy because we lack sympathy for those impoverished people, or are we lazy because we are spiritually impoverished ourselves?

Are we following Jesus and serving others out of empathy, compassion, and love, the kind only God can give, or are we following a god we call *service*? Have we diminished the rest of the gospel because we are conforming to the current social justice–oriented society, or do we know, recognize, love, and teach the entire gospel message?

Consider the words of A.W. Tozer in his book *The Knowledge of the Holy*:

> Always the most revealing thing about the Church is her idea of God, just as her most significant message is what she says about Him or leaves unsaid, for her silence is often more eloquent than her speech. She can never escape the self-disclosure of her witness concerning God.[6]

If our beliefs about God and our submission to him are only select portions of the gospel, we have created and served a false god.

* * *

I don't know many of the answers to the questions in this chapter. I don't want to cause anger or pain for those who are always smiling and talking with strangers. I often wish I could be more like you. I admire and respect the person the Lord created you to be. You are the ones who provide sunshine to the struggling on cloudy days. You are the ones who bring much hope to many people. I know the body of Christ needs individuals like you. I know people like you have sharpened me.

I truly hope the acts of service our churches are doing are making disciples and furthering the gospel message. I hope I was merely receiving condemnation from Satan and that our churches are genuinely brokenhearted for the lost, the poor, the hungry, and the oppressed. I hope our intent is not to boost numbers for numbers' sake. I hope we are solid in the Word and eager to share its message because the Lord asks us to do so.

* * *

Maybe some people will find comfort in this chapter because they're backward like me, a disciplined follower of Jesus who would rather try to breathe underwater than go door-to-door handing out pamphlets. Maybe they are faithfully serving the poor in spirit by offering their time to write a book about all their mistakes and the hope God brings. I truly believe there is a place in the body of Christ for each of us. I truly believe we can all serve others and further the gospel by being devoted to his Word without having to completely scrap the specs God used when he created us. I believe God is pleased with the creativity he used when he knit each of us in the womb. Why else would he have created us different if it wasn't on purpose?

How do I obey the Lord without conforming to the good person Satan wants me to be? How do I attempt to serve as an imitator of Jesus, disciplined in the commissions in the Word? I wait on the Lord. I know the Shepherd's voice and act on his instruction. The Lord wants me to be this odd creature that follows him as though my actions are notes in his symphony. I'm not given his sheet music; I only know his style. I am to pay rigorous attention to his every move, playing the exact notes he requires when he signals me. I know his previous creations, and I'm not supposed to play a solo. Only he knows what is required to make the music beautiful. Only he knows what to play in order to bring others into the orchestra. He has made various instruments that produce different sounds. When they are each following his lead, heads turn in awe of this creative composer.

I will not leave this orchestra for another. I will not lay down the instrument I play and take up one of a fellow musician. I will not turn my eyes from the conductor, lest I forget why I was created.

CHAPTER SIX

YOU'RE A FAILURE

Little children, guard yourselves from idols.

—1 John 5:21

Have you ever been told to get out your paper and pencil and then realize you didn't arrive with either? I haven't, not this gal. I'm the type who predicts the items required for an upcoming task and shows up with at least one of each. Always prepared, storms can't catch me off guard. I'm like the protagonist waiting in the chair for the villain to arrive. I laugh as the rain begins to drop and proclaim, *I knew you'd come, you little moisture-filled army. I check the weather every morning. You're right on time.* I have been known to make an occasional mistake, like the *one* time I showed up at the grocery store on senior citizens day. They haven't seen me there on a Thursday since. I'm not going to lie, there's a weird sort of internal pleasure I receive from being prepared. It's as satisfying as a piece of chocolate cake. The satisfaction isn't a comparison thing or laughing at those who are ill-equipped. It's just the high of defeating a task.

For me, responsibility, preparedness, and intelligence feel like they go hand-in-hand. For instance, when burning firewood in a woodstove, the wood needs to be properly seasoned in order to burn clean, reducing the amount of creosote buildup in the stovepipe and CO_2 emissions. To properly season wood, the tree should be cut, split, and stacked for around a year prior to use.[1] If old man winter approaches and my firewood has just been split, I am unprepared. I could also appear ignorant, because I must not know that burning green wood is unsafe, doesn't burn as hot, and is a major pain to keep lit. Like a kid who shows up to school without his or her homework, I'm responsible enough to have firewood but not responsible or intelligent enough to complete the task correctly.

For most of my life, I've sat in the captain's chair and landed my plane perfectly according to plan and schedule. I never doubted the success that would follow someone who is actively pursuing achievement. I was ready to work diligently for my cake and eat it too.

Well, at least that's the person I used to be—the person I was when I was in control.

* * *

Being the mother of three kids, I can't believe people trusted me to babysit their children when I was young. I guess, to my credit, the kids were always alive and well when the parents returned. One black eye in all those years isn't too bad of a reputation. And if the older boy had any coordination whatsoever, he would have caught the perfectly thrown football with his hands instead of his face. It was pure relief, however, when I came of age and took the title "sandwich artist" instead of babysitter. It's a little strange that I was paid more for tossing lunch meat on bread than for keeping baby humans alive. Our desire for a good sandwich must be pretty high.

With the exception of a single semester, I held at least one part-time job through high school, four years of college, and our first year of marriage. I came by my intense work ethic honestly, from my parents. While maintaining a full-time job, my dad deconstructed two homes and reused whatever materials he could to build a dream home. Don't think tiny—we're talking a 3,000-square-foot house with some fancy crown molding and fluted columns. I remember my mom being in her heels after work helping my dad brace the two-story living room wall. I think I also recall some select words that day, but we can leave that part out. My dad would tell me I only had to work with him half the day, and I could pick which half—whichever 12 hours I wanted to work. Needless to say, my parents valued a good work ethic. I followed right in line, dotting my i's and crossing my t's. I was a prepared, intelligent, hard-working girl. I was on track for what the world would have declared a success. I was ready for the heavy lifting of life.

All was smooth sailing until that day the omniscient God told me not to get a job. I can count on one hand the times in my life when I had full confidence in God's direction. To not seek employment at this time was one of them. My husband and I had just moved back to my hometown where he had been hired as a youth pastor. It was curious, this unemployment quest the Lord was speaking of, but I assumed it would be short-lived. I obeyed the Lord in his prompting, no matter how foreign it seemed. For the first two months, I busied myself, stripping endless wallpaper from the plaster of the house we were to inhabit and weeding through piles of our combined junk. I stayed busy until a stomach virus demanded I could not leave the couch. The virus lasted nine months and ended up being our firstborn child. I wasn't exactly enthused by the surprise. Having children this early was not part of my plan. In the middle of the night, after I'd made another violent trip to the bathroom, I looked over at my husband, asleep in bed, and realized what the Lord was teaching me: It was time for me to depend on someone other than myself. The Lord knew this hard-working girl could not do pregnancy and maintain a job. The Lord knew that had this baby never existed, I would have eventually grabbed the reins and demanded my priorities. The Lord knew I must be forced to learn the lesson of trust.

It's too bad I'm so hard-headed. Otherwise, much of my refining might have been a quicker process. The Lord broke me in slowly, providing our housing those first two years and providing a decent salary. We were able to pay off the majority of my husband's student loan and begin a retirement savings account. We were being responsible. The remaining income supported our typical low-key lifestyle, and all was well. I wasn't itching for control because the Lord seemed to be getting things done. We were not climbing any corporate ladders or gaining massive wealth, but I was trusting the Lord. I saw our situation as a brief respite before we tackled life head on.

We must have made a decent first step because it wasn't long before God called us to go deeper into dependence on him. From his prompting, we moved without employment, with our year-old child, to join the process of planting a church two hours away. My husband was brought on as the co-planter and associate pastor. When planting a new church, it can take many years before there are resources that can support pastors full-time, so my husband sought additional employment. He quickly got a job at a t-shirt printing company. We emptied what little retirement savings we had and kept our eyes focused on fulfilling the task the Lord set before us. I told myself it was okay to be irresponsible in this way because the Lord would make up for these steps backward down the road. With my husband making just above minimum wage, I would have relished the opportunity to join the workforce, but the Lord had not released me to do so. The world would have said we were some of the hardest working fools around, never idle but not gaining much to show for it. We were two ambitious, college-degree-holding adults making less than a first-year teacher. But shopping at Goodwill meant we were cool, so we fit in pretty well.

About three years later, little had changed. My husband had been given a salaried position by another company, but it was an entry-level position at a company that was struggling to stay afloat. The head pastor at the church was now salaried, and although the church was growing by the hundreds, it didn't seem my husband would get to that place for quite some time. My husband and I had been out of college for seven years and five years, respectively, but we had very little to show for that time. We were debt-free and responsible with the finances we had, but there wasn't a penny of retirement to our names. We didn't own a house, couldn't afford our own healthcare, and qualified for our church's outreach programs. According to my internal order of operations, everything about our situation screamed *failure.* I kept telling myself to hold on, that the Lord would show up soon, but I must have subconsciously set an alarm clock for God for when our time for lateral movements had expired. The bell had been ringing for too long, and I slowly started to lay down the shield of faith. As I watched our friends go through life the way I had imagined we would—taking family vacations, buying minivans, and owning a home—I felt betrayed by God.

I'll break it down in simple form, but just keep in mind the image of that prepared, hard-working girl. We had no savings or emergency fund in the bank, we had no retirement, we weren't working our way up in a company, our cars did not have adequate airbags in case of an accident, we couldn't start our children in any classes (gymnastics, dance, piano), the government provided our healthcare, and we had hocked all our old jewelry. We were trying to spread the gospel and were rewarded by living paycheck to paycheck. Where was the Lord? Was he running this plane on autopilot? I was angry at the slowness of his timeline. I was confused as to why those surrendering everything to him—our family—were the ones driving the clunkers. I was tired of the Lord making me look like a failure. I was tired of trusting the Lord to manage our lives.

The enemy knows how much I loathe the feeling of failure. He was ready and able to send arrows soaring as soon as my shield was down. He would use our lack of financial resources as constant evidence of what a disappointment I had become. I remember needing to go to a store on Christmas Eve and having an elderly employee greet us at the door. I remember hearing the enemy whisper, *That will be you someday. You'll have to be in a place like this until you die just to pay your bills.* I should have fired back at him about how thankful I would be to have a job and live in such a wonderful country, but instead I took the shame the enemy fed me. I began believing his lies because the facts of the matter pointed at the lies being true.

Did my husband ever become a full-time pastor? No, but the fella the church hired a month after my husband voluntarily stepped away was given a high enough salary to support his family of six. I don't say that to cast blame on the church, but it may shed more light on the healing I needed from the sin of taking offense. It felt like a slap in the face. Maybe I didn't see it as the Lord slapping us, but he was sitting there allowing it to happen. Thus the lie I carried on my shoulders every day: *You have followed God with all your might, and he made a mockery of you.*

* * *

I never dreamed I'd consider myself a failure while following Jesus. In the world's eyes, we had sacrificed much in pursuing his will. In my ignorance, I had not offered it all. I neglected to lay down my idol of success. My actions in following God appeared to be all in, but the situation proved that my heart needed more faith. I had followed God into the desert, but I continued to grumble at his leading. He daily provided our manna, but we were unable to store any for the next day. When emergencies occurred, the body of Christ had taken care of our needs, which was God bringing forth water from the rock. Yet I continued to test the Lord. He wasn't providing the Promised Land I assumed we would receive.

* * *

I'll bet the wisdom in Matthew 6:24 rings some bells: "No one can serve two masters; for either he will hate the one and love the other, or he will be devoted to one and despise the other. You cannot serve God and wealth."

How in the world was I attempting to serve wealth while earning a big goose egg? Try this phrasing: You cannot serve God and the American dream. By being at home with my children, I was serving the Lord because that was the calling he had put on my life. To my chagrin, he hadn't made the other paths straight. But I began despising service to the Lord because it did not produce the wealth, comfort, and self-respect I was devoted to achieving. Society viewed my situation as failing, as did I. I thought I had laid down my nets to follow Jesus, but he was shining a light on the idol I held with a death grip. The merciful, sovereign Lord was trying to reveal the sacred pillars and altars I had constructed—ones with stars and stripes, altars with treasures on earth, pillars holding the pursuit of happiness.

I believed I was a failure because I had adopted a type of prosperity gospel. Having everything flourish for me and my family somehow became synonymous with following the will of God. I saw the riches of David and Job as possibilities for my future, not the possibility of being crucified. I didn't think I'd dance in the streets, pour out the bottles of perfume, or be exiled to a tiny island. The subtle message of guaranteed prosperity had been a false teacher. With awareness of the idol I held, I had to choose to lay it down if I were to continue following him. I had to trust that the future he desired, whether crucified or flourishing, was better than my own hopes and dreams. For the love of the Lord, I had to put my hand to the plow and not look back. I had to be willing to face the lie that I was a failure and smile, knowing I had chosen to serve one Master.

* * *

What do you think? What exactly did you picture when you became a Christian? Was it someone who surrendered control of everything to the Lord—time, money, reputation, talents? Do we as Christian Americans anticipate suffering? Do we have a unique stumbling block to our faith?

What's the most comical point of all this? We think we can control our lives, but that's foolishness. We can be wise, faithfully trusting in the sovereignty of the Lord, but it may not look like wisdom to the world.

I'm a big fan of how John Piper describes the devil's work, "People sometimes ask why, if Satan is real, we don't see more demon possession and exorcisms in America. I have an idea. Satan holds American Christianity so tightly in the vice-grip of comfort and wealth that he's not about to tip his hand with too much demonic tomfoolery."[2] We can become so fat and happy sensually that we are oblivious to our own spiritual starvation. I believed I was poor, pitiful, and failing because I wasn't moving closer to a life of comfort. I hope this is the most childish thing I will ever do, for it is so far from the truth. We have freely been given the peace that surpasses understanding, an inheritance that cannot be destroyed, and access to an everlasting God upon whom we may put our trust. Only a fool hesitates in relinquishing control to the Lord Almighty. Only a fool determines those who follow the Lord to be failures.

* * *

We are now 10 years out from that day the Lord told me not to get a job. Great progress has been made in my heart for many of the lies I believed. Other than being a wife, mother, and a few side-gigs, I have only been released by the Lord to write this book. Maybe the Lord has asked that this book be written now, on a computer borrowed from the church, because the message needs to be spoken from one who has not known tremendous prosperity. If my family were affluent, rubbing elbows with all the bigwigs, maybe I'd suggest that you hold on until the Lord knocks your socks off. Maybe that's not the heart change he wishes for you or for me.

Many are the distractions the enemy can use on us when it comes to chasing success. I may never own a company or be able to retire, but I'm finished being a slave to Satan's standards of achievement. I have an inheritance that will never spoil. I will spend my days praising the Lord. I have been clothed in righteousness. The world can keep its rags and its riches.

CHAPTER SEVEN

YOU'RE POOR

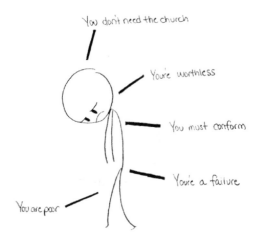

He who trusts in his riches will fall, but the righteous will flourish like the green leaf.

—Proverbs 11:28

I'm choking back tears as I drive our squealing car. My daughter is squished in the backseat, trying to keep peace between her two fussy brothers. Financial advisor Dave Ramsey is on the radio, the income of his guests reminding me of how little we have. I had tried to spend the day comforting a friend, but the sentences produced from sleep deprivation didn't seem to make any sense. The above-average brain I once had must be dead. I'm on my way home to clean the maggots out of the car's floor board from an apple core that disappeared under the seat. It decomposed on a Mother's Day picture that should have been displayed on the mantel. I had cleaned the car two weeks earlier when I finally found the tubs of sour cream I knew I had purchased. Trapped in the trunk, the heat of the summer burst the containers. I thought the smell was from a missing sippy cup. Whatever I aspired to be, this was not it. I didn't aspire to be someone whose main success revolved around whether they showered that day. Nor did I aspire to be someone who picked maggots out of their car because they didn't notice rotting fruit among the other filth. I didn't aspire to be poor.

I had hoped to be better off. I should have been the one on the Dave Ramsey show, celebrating our debt-free life at age 30. I should be showered and dressed, bringing food and a gift to my friend in need. The paid-for home that I'm driving to should be spacious and in order. My children should be relaxed, each having their own comfortable seat in my huge, clean SUV. I should have picked them up at their prestigious daycare after a successful day at my very important job. I aspired to have more.

* * *

You're probably thinking that you just read this chapter and that this author is getting a little redundant. You'll have to forgive the areas that seem repetitive. By focusing on myself and doubting God, a few lies I believed seemed to hold hands in order to achieve their goal. Believing I was a failure led to a depressed life full of self-pity. Believing I was poor aided in the conviction of failure, but it also produced another result.

* * *

I don't believe it's a sin to desire nice things. I can't picture God being upset about us wanting a dependable car in which to transport our children. I can't picture him being angry at the larger homes people purchase, knowing they'll need enough space in the living room to host a weekly Bible study. I would never claim that poverty points to sin or that all followers of Jesus should lead radical lives of poverty. That message is too close to conformity, in my opinion. The Lord needs followers everywhere. How will those in a gated community experience Jesus from their neighbors if God has not placed one of his children among them? I can personally attest to the amazing blessing of those in affluence who are following the Lord and give selflessly out of the resources in their care.

The very important point of the matter is one of the heart or one of the hands. Whether we believe we are poor or wealthy, do we lift our open hands to the Lord, knowing whatever we have is his, or are we tight-fisted and self-absorbed? Do we need all the financial and material wealth we possess? If we don't, could it have been given to us in order for us to give it away? Is it possible that the money spent to purchase the thing in the corner collecting dust could have blessed another brother or sister in Christ? As followers of Jesus, what type of giver should we become?

* * *

It's a lot of fun to earn the big bucks. For my last two years of high school, I was making $11 per hour at a wonderful company. This job was many moons ago, but it's still much more than minimum wage today. I brought home a bigger paycheck than any high schooler needs, so I gave a lot of it away. I'd buy treasured gifts for loved ones, no matter the cost, and donate to charities. I faithfully tithed to our church and anonymously gave to those in need. These gifts were a blessing to those on the receiving end, but I loved being part of the giving. One of my favorite things in the world is to show love in this manner. I didn't desire recognition or praise. The joy of witnessing the reaction of someone being blessed beyond what they could have dreamed was enough reward.

I continued this mindset and these actions through college as much as opportunity presented itself. My finances weren't quite as abundant, but the thrill of blessing someone was just as fulfilling. Every once in a while, I'd encounter an individual who would take without question or gratitude. Fighting the feeling of being taken advantage of, I had to allow the Lord to work on my heart in those scenarios. If God provided the resource or item in the first place, he'd either provide it again or I didn't need it.

Smitten with love or something like that, I met my husband in college and we married a few months after

I graduated. Although he had hundreds of amazing character traits, he was just learning the skill of money management. Like many young American couples, we found student loan debt to be the worst wedding gift. We took off across the country on an adventure of travel, employment, and ministry and began paying off the debt. Four years later, we made our final payment on the $15,000, and we were debt-free. It was time to live again!

Except it wasn't. I wouldn't say that kids are expensive, but when you haven't been raised around them, the learning curve can be costly. For instance, when your firstborn child won't sleep when placed on her back on a cold, hard mattress in a room by herself, you're willing to spend every penny you have for a contraption that will make her love bedtime. Maybe you decide to try the swing with the soothing sounds and vibrations and the 50 D batteries you have to replace every week. Maybe the tiny bassinet would make her more comfortable, but what do you do when she outgrows it? Maybe you just put her bed beside yours, burp her well, and let her sleep on her stomach. I felt tremendous guilt over this until we both woke well-rested the next morning. Godspeed to every parent of a newborn.

If you survive the infant stage, you'll soon encounter the first time the child displays intense joy over a toy. You may think of this toy as obnoxious and a waste of money, but instead, you give the shirt off your back to make her wish come true. You'd give this kid the moon if she wanted it and you had a lasso. Although you love your subsequent children just as much, buying the toy is a rookie mistake. Depending on how much you fell for the puppy eyes of child number one, by kid two or three, your heart is tender toward their request for a split second before you remember tripping over hundreds of toys in the house, and you quickly crush their hopes and dreams. Parents who have had child number one around long enough know that a birthday or Christmas, with its millions of toys, is always just around the corner.

It's safe to say that my husband and I made all the first-time parent trial and error mistakes. We both have huge hearts when it comes to making a kid happy. When our firstborn was around three years old, something in me began to change. Strapping my daughter into her cheap, Walmart car seat, I fought off the heartbreak of not being able to provide a "safer," more comfortable mode of transportation. Watching my friends take their children to dance classes, I'd tell myself that maybe next year we could take our child. I'd buy toys at consignment sales and hope she didn't notice when pieces were missing. The child had everything she needed, but I wanted to provide her with more.

I guess I was used to the feelings once we had our first son. The kids enjoyed the library programs, going to the park, and grandma's swimming pool. Truly, at such a young age, they didn't know any different, but I did. I knew we'd be forced to sell one of our internal organs if our kids wanted to participate in gymnastics or karate. I knew the shoes and clothes they wore were purchased from second-hand stores. I knew their vacations to grandparents' houses weren't trips to Disney World. I knew their birthday parties would never involve a bounce house or a venue. I knew we were poor.

Money hadn't affected me before my children were born. As long as we paid the bills and maintained a little cushion in the bank, I didn't think about this green god. As long as we were comfortable, I could care less if an article of clothing was a certain brand. I didn't need the most expensive of anything as long as the item served its purpose. This compulsion to want more for my children was different, however. Even though it wasn't a sinful desire in itself, I didn't notice when it shifted to jealousy of other, more affluent families. I didn't notice the discontentment it bred within me. I didn't notice the self-absorption it created. I didn't notice my hands slowly turning into clenched fists.

I began to reluctantly host the weekly Bible study, bitter at what it would cost. We continued to tithe, but I found myself wanting to reduce the amount. I stopped spending time with certain friends because I hated hearing about their family excursions. My anger about items that got broken accidentally grew because I knew how much it would cost to replace them. I was absorbed with thinking of ways we could earn more money while not directly disobeying the Lord's call on our lives. What I desired lacked the appearance of being sinful, but my heart was full of greed, jealousy, anger, and self-pity. My once open hands were closed and withdrawn because I believed the lies that were thrown at me. Leave it to a serpent to use your love for your child against you.

* * *

Reflecting on this time in my life, I can't think of a more appropriate analogy regarding my behavior than a slave Jesus spoke of in the book of Matthew:

> For this reason the kingdom of heaven may be compared to a king who wished to settle accounts with his slaves. When he had begun to settle them, one who owed him ten thousand talents was brought to him. But since he did not have the means to repay, his lord commanded him to be sold, along with his wife and children and all that he had, and repayment to be made. So the slave fell to the ground and prostrated himself before him, saying, "Have patience with me and I will repay you everything." And the lord of that slave felt compassion and released him and forgave him the debt. But that slave went out and found one of his fellow slaves who owed him a hundred denarii; and he seized him and began to choke him, saying, "Pay back what you owe." So his fellow slave fell to the ground and began to plead with him, saying, "Have patience with me and I will repay you." But he was unwilling and went and threw him in prison until he should pay back what was owed. So when his fellow slaves saw what had happened, they were deeply grieved and came and reported to their lord all that had happened. Then summoning him, his lord said to him, "You wicked slave, I

forgave you all that debt because you pleaded with me. Should you not also have had mercy on your fellow slave, in the same way that I had mercy on you?"

—Matt. 18:23–33

The parable was spoken to represent God's (the king's) forgiveness of repentant sinners and the anger he has toward those who have been forgiven much (the slave the king forgave) but who refuse to offer forgiveness to others. Although this parable clearly revolves around forgiveness, I see myself in the forgiven slave. I see myself as a person who has been given more than I could possibly deserve and then turned to leave, clenching my fists. The slave lacked mercy and compassion for others even after he had been forgiven. The kindness he received did not penetrate his heart of stone. The slave was unchanged by the king's mercy.

According to national averages, my family lived at the poverty level, but we often forget what a privilege it is to live in this country. We were "impoverished," but we owned two automobiles, had a beautiful roof over our heads, could feed our children, and had a consistent income. We live in a country where the items at consignment stores are hardly used. Our cities and towns have playgrounds for our children. Our libraries have more books and programs than our families could ever complete. It's not a difficult task to find a bicycle for your child at a yard sale for a few pennies. On any given day, I'm almost certain you can find an event that is giving out free pizza. My selfish heart wasn't created out of a situation of true poverty. That concept was a lie. My selfish heart was created out of preference and believing that I knew what was best for our family. The Lord had provided for our needs and then some, but I turned and left, choosing a greedy heart over one of gladness.

* * *

I won't fib and say that I was able make an about-face as soon as my folly was exposed. It took almost a year for God to break down my love of stuff. I've had to practice trusting him, believing that he loves my children more than I ever could and that only he knows what is best for them. I had to trust him that the accumulation of stuff and activities did not directly equate to a successful child who is loved by God. I had to trust that the Lord had my family's best interest in mind.

It's amazing how the hands and the heart are connected. The more my heart softened, the more my hands opened. The more my hands opened, the more peace filled my heart. I find it hilarious that being on the other side of this self-centered season, all I want to do is give our things away. We have too much. Our stuff is a burden to maintain. I'm hunting down others who could use the items and giving freely. The less stuff we have to maintain, the more time we have to spend with friends and family. With gladness in our hearts, we share whatever we can with the body of Christ. By the grace of God, my heart has been made cheerful again, because I know that no matter what the world says, a child of the King has reason to give.

CHAPTER EIGHT

YOU'D BE HAPPIER WITH SOMEONE ELSE

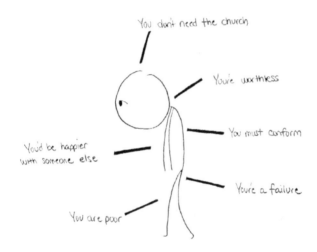

And the world held its breath
And then one by one the stars began to applaud
We were the greatest thing they'd seen
From here and afar.

—"Crooner," Ben Sollee

It was October in Kentucky, heaven on earth. The song lyrics opening this chapter serenaded us as we took the floor for our first dance as husband and wife. We were married on my parents' farm with the full moon as our witness. It was humbling to see what amazing friends and family we collectively shared. I remember feeling quite unworthy. The food was amazing, the crickets loud, and the twinkling lights even louder. The night was perfect, so much so that I wondered if angels were in attendance.

Our wedding was quite the opposite of when I first met my husband. Hands down, he took me on the worst dates I had ever experienced. The first evening, he forgot he had previously committed to playing in a basketball tournament. I sat in a crowd of strangers and watched as he received a technical foul from the bench (he still claims the ref was a joke). When we continued the "date" portion, he forgot his wallet, twice. The second date was a surprise trip to the ice skating rink with some kids he babysat. At that time, babysitting and ice skating were neck-and-neck at the bottom of my list of enjoyable activities. The night concluded with us driving separate vehicles. He drove a car full of children, and I chauffeured the SUV full of their tipsy parents. I remember looking at the cash tip in my hand at the end of the date and thinking that this type of ending usually doesn't qualify as one you'd tell your children someday. I guess you could assume that I stuck with this guy out of loneliness and desperation, at least that's what I tell him when he has me in a headlock.

But the truth was that curiosity got the best of me as I began to see in this man a heart like no other. He was noble and honest. Where I was raised, I was used to seeing pride in men or at least false pride, but he possessed neither. His care for others was always genuine. I could trust him to defend me, physically and emotionally. He was as fierce as a lion and as gentle as a lamb. He was patient, not easily angered, and did not keep track of wrongs. He was quite unlike me, and for that, I respected him.

I'd say it was our mutual hobbies that kept us going strong. But you are already aware that our bliss hit a rock in the road. Far be it for Satan to neglect a marriage when attempting to turn a believer from the Lord. I wanted to abandon my husband because I began believing he had abandoned me. The lie felt like a spider web methodically constructed over many years. I found myself hesitating in my vulnerability toward him because my trust had somehow diminished. My teammate had become my opponent. I was tangled in the spider's web.

* * *

The long list of similarities my husband and I shared is equal to the list of differences. For instance, he is a right-brained, extroverted, water-sport and Kung-Fu-loving dude. I am not. He sees the whole picture; I see the details. He utilizes trial and error to solve problems; I spend time with pencil and paper. He'd be happy traveling the world; I'm a homebody. He can explain an event in fifteen minutes; I'll tell you what you need to know in one. He is sarcastic; okay, we might share that. Most often, we worked well as a team. Together, being different, we saw a more complete picture. Our typical frustrations were childish. When we attempted to complete a task together, he did not share my sense of efficiency and speed, and I did not share his patience. But since both of us tend to be peacemakers, I can't say that any serious arguments ever arose.

But I didn't consider how my husband's occupation would affect us once we were married. We both loved Jesus, and he knew he was to spend his days in discipleship and teaching. That sounded great to me. I'd see him at five o'clock after I had completed my day's work. But then there was that alternate prompting of the Lord for my work to be at home—a wife and mother—a pastor's wife and pastor's kids' mother. I guess I put those on my own pedestals since the inadequacy followed the revelation. Once we began our journey in ministry, I started feeling some pangs of guilt. I wasn't like the typical pastor's wife. I didn't smile non-stop, shake everyone's hand, organize the baby showers, and play the piano. I couldn't sing and wasn't equipped to handle all the female church members' issues. I was content being the ninja wife, sneaking in the service, hiding in the shadows, then sneaking back out. I have literally spin-moved someone on the way to the bathroom. He is still alive and will be my witness. I'm sure he remembers since I yelled "spin move" while doing so. Put me on the team for building projects or mowing the lawn, but please don't make me have hundreds of small-talk conversations.

I felt as though I held my husband back in ministry. If I were as outgoing as he is, maybe the flock under his care would multiply. I questioned the Lord's wisdom and my husband's choice of a wife. He hated when I spoke of this and never desired for me to be something I wasn't, but I often thought a different woman would be a more suitable helper. I saw my character traits as a hindrance instead of a help.

With reassurance from my mate, I attempted to fight the self-doubt. Maybe the Kung Fu lover married the ninja wife because of her ridiculous skills. I tried to rearrange my thinking—my main goal was to be supportive of my husband, not to fulfill the same calling as he had. I stayed at home most often during the week and attempted to complete every chore so he would be able to rest upon arrival. He was working two and sometimes three jobs to support us, allowing me plenty of time to manage the home. From grocery shopping to painting, there really wasn't a chore I wasn't willing to complete. I'd mow the grass with the baby monitor on my hip, fix dinner, and then wash and wax the car for my own enjoyment. I'm not a hard-core brute of a woman. I just get bored sitting still. Even when he was tired when he got home, I was given plenty of mommy time-outs to recharge after a day with children. We were making this work, for the most part.

During this time, I learned that my husband's mind was five miles ahead of his current setting. The reason he'd leave his dishes in the living room was because he was thinking about the person he needed to call when he got to work. The reason he'd forget to call the home insurance guy was because of work calls. The reason the house lights were left on was because his mind was already at his next destination. The reason his shoes were left in the doorway was because he thought he was coming right back for them. I would pick up the dishes, turn out the lights, move his shoes, and remind him the next morning to make the phone call. I knew my husband was overwhelmed with the responsibilities he had. For me to pick up whatever slack he left behind set me back a measly two minutes. *It's no big deal. It's no big deal,* I'd try to convince myself as I tripped over the shoes while 30 weeks pregnant. It's no big deal that I pick up after the kids and my husband. I loathed the nagging wife, so I tried desperately to be the opposite, subtly making suggestions here and there but mostly trying to swallow the frustration. Sometimes, he would attempt to be more courteous, but it appeared he was exchanging one grievance for another. I knew my husband was not intentionally thinking of me when he neglected things around the house. But that was the problem; he didn't seem to be thinking of me. I didn't know how to allow him to relax at home and not be upset when it felt like he had trampled on my space—the place I worked all day to improve. Then it happened, a voice small and sly began to repeat, *He doesn't care about you.*

I knew this statement was a lie, but my supportive arguments were losing credibility. The busier our lives became, the more tasks were shifted to my responsibility. I didn't mind taking out the trash, but as I dragged the cans to the curb in the snow, I'd have to fight off the voices that said, *If he cared about you, he would have remembered to do this.* My husband wasn't wasting time golfing or going to bars with his buddies. He was working a depleting job and using his free time to prepare for church services. He was working as hard as he could to get us to a place where he would be responsible for only one job, his ministry, and could spend more time at home. Even though he was giving 100 percent to be my hero, it was all I could do to fight the lie that he was not. Absent from him most of the time, I tried to ignore the frustrating reminders he'd leave behind. I looked like *Sméagol* (later called Gollum), the psychosis of a desperate being using whatever was left of her sanity to continue the right quest.

Then came our third child. I suddenly couldn't juggle as many balls as I had in the past. I needed my husband to take up some of the slack. I needed him to be my hero—to take out the trash before it overflowed, to plan a date night, to appear as though he had it all together because I knew I was falling to pieces. He would help where he could, but most often, he wasn't there. As he would head to church on Sunday to prepare, I'd count it as another day that I was alone raising the kids. Dragging three kids to church by myself wasn't exactly a vacation. Once there, the children were still under my care as my husband went about his duties. *He can't help you even when he's present. You are miserable and he gets to do what he loves. He's abandoned you,* the words would cycle through my mind.

Our usual evenings included my husband arriving just as dinner was going on the table. It was a loud meal shared with some child who eventually cried, followed by cleaning the dishes and taking care of the kids. I'd take a break on the couch, folding laundry or feeding the infant, while my husband put the older children to bed. Typically, he fell asleep with them and wouldn't wake up until I was brushing my teeth, ready to turn in for the night. I was alone during the day, assisted for a brief time during dinner, and then alone again. I was weary of the absence. I needed a helpmate in my world of influence and a friend with whom I could share life, but my husband was far off in another galaxy. *Maybe someone else could be your helpmate!* I'd push the thought out as I continued each day longing for someone to share these burdens. I was desperate for the company of my husband, but the longer the loneliness dragged on, the more I began desiring the company of any husband. The question became louder and repeated more often, attempting to lure me away: *Perhaps someone else could be your hero!*

That's when Satan blew his cover. That's when C.S. Lewis's Uncle Screwtape would have lit into his demon nephew for taking the lies too far. If the demons take their influence too far, their actions become obvious and they expose themselves, he'd instruct. You see, I'm a "go down with the ship" kind of gal. You'd have to drag me off the boat to get me to leave my crew. The idea of other men being able to soothe any woes of mine was a joke. First, it's not as if another fella wouldn't have a whole host of baggage in tow. Second, take two seconds to come back to reality. My husband is not my opponent; he is my teammate. He has been working endlessly for the team, the team I care for each day. We are both on the same team and want what's best for it. We are companions, helpmates, and our battle is not against each other.

Satan's lies were dragged into the light, but I still didn't trust my condition enough to self-soothe. The desperate feeling of loneliness combined with the other lies surrounding me had pushed me to the end of my rope. I needed the Lord. I needed my husband. It was time to see what this team was made of.

* * *

I remember sitting at our dining room table one morning, my face torn with emotion. I had hinted at my frustrations with the Lord—disappointments with the church, my husband, and our financial situation in the past—but it would have taken a book to explain their depth. How do I tell my husband that I've wondered if the stranger on the street would take better care of me than he was? How does that come across in a way that begs him to rescue me instead of running away? We took the entire day to weed out what I was trying to say. No matter how I rehearsed my words, they felt like knives when they exited my mouth. When I looked up to see my husband's reaction, he appeared unmoved—unmoved in the sense that he wasn't angry with me. His teammate had finally exposed her true condition, and she was bleeding out. I was weak and ashamed. I had allowed the years to wound me. I had failed at being his helpmate. I had laid a dilemma on the poor chap—continue the mission and sacrifice the girl, or abort mission and save her.

It wasn't like what you see in the movies. The climax of our story didn't end with the prince immediately throwing everything to the wayside, grabbing the injured princess and rushing her to safety. There was hesitation—a hesitation that I tried not to mistake for a lack of love. The mission my husband would need to abort was the only one he had ever known. When he was 17 years old, the Lord had asked him to work in the church, and he had been faithful to that calling every day since. But one of his flock was about to be eaten by wolves. Attempting to not be an inconvenience to others, I had allowed my wounds to go too far. I couldn't drag myself back to the Shepherd.

A counselor may have helped, but I needed my husband. I needed his actual presence with me to help fight the lies I wrestled with regarding him. With my husband being the sole bread winner, he could not quit his paying job. The only way he would have time to tend to our marriage, to shepherd his wife, was to step away from his position at the church.

A few weeks after I exposed the situation, my husband stepped down from formal ministry. I told everyone it was my fault, that I couldn't press on with things the way they were. I hated every moment of stealing my husband's dream from him. He assured me that saving our marriage was, and should be, the most important relationship to him after his own relationship with the Lord. I also hated feeling like I could be tampering with God's desire for this church, but it was evident from the God-fearing men who stood ready to assume the responsibilities that God could take care of his church. Two women comforted me in the days and weeks that followed. Both had been divorced. They commended me for the courage it took to be honest with my husband. They said they wished they had done the same.

* * *

I don't know of many arranged marriages in America. Most of us choose our spouses by having enough similarities and attraction toward one another that we think we can make it through the long haul. Many do not. How do we get from friends to enemies, teammates to opponents? Do we start to hate the differences instead of seeing them as ways to fill our voids? Do we allow pride to fill our ears, removing the ability of iron sharpening iron? Do we forget the Lord's ability to make us more like him if we are devoted to prayer and humility? Do we know that our critical insults break down the team, but we would rather defend ourselves? When do we realize that seeing our spouse as our opponent is exactly what Satan desires?

Would the words we use with our spouse be different if we maintained a teammate mentality? Would we seek to help one another more because helping the other person is helping our team? What about in baseball? Does a pitcher who throws the ball all willy-nilly not affect the entire team? If the left fielder decides to sit and pout, does that not affect the team? If the shortstop is drunk, if the first baseman doesn't show up, if the right fielder hurls critical insults, if the catcher makes no effort, is the team winning? If our goal is to win this game of life and marriage, does it not profit us to remember our teammate?

* * *

By the skin of my teeth, our marriage was redeemed. It doesn't mean either of us is perfect, but when conflict arises, I'm much more prone to want to change my own heart issues. I see each conflict as an opportunity to improve the function of the team instead of an opportunity to take offense. My goal for each day is still the same—to remember my husband is on my team. Since he's not a task-oriented person, he still forgets to take out the trash now and again. The difference is that I won't allow myself to be persuaded to believe that the incomplete task is a display of his indifference toward me. We have spent enough devoted time together that I can recognize and laugh at this implication.

As Christians, the marriage of a husband and a wife has great purpose—to represent Christ and the church (Eph. 5:22–33). What do our marriages teach the world about Jesus and his beloved bride? Does Jesus look like a man that would lay down his life for the one he loves? Does the church look like it is so devoted to him that it is willing to leave behind the world and its fleshly desires? Will Satan one day attempt to accuse us of not knowing God since our earthly marriage represented neither Jesus nor his church?

We need the grace of God to change our self-centered hearts. And in turn, we need to show that grace to our spouses. We need to remember the wisdom of God in joining a husband and a wife together as a team. As followers of Christ, that team needs to keep in mind its witness to the world.

CHAPTER NINE

YOU'RE A GONER

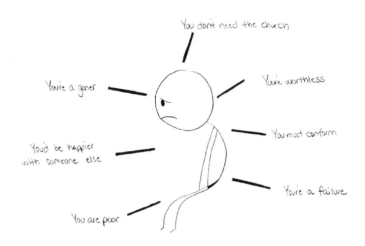

But some will courageously escape
The seductive voice with a heart of faith
While walkin' that line back home
—"Farther Along," Josh Garrels*

---

* "Farther Along"—Josh Garrels ©2011 Josh Garrels / Small Voice Music. From "Love & War & The Sea In Between," June 15, 2011.

I sat in my car in the parking lot feeling like I could complete two marathons. The adrenaline racing through my veins was unlike anything I had ever felt. It was dark out, so I didn't hesitate to reason with myself out loud. I needed to be talked down. I'm not sure what I needed to be talked down from, but I didn't feel stable. The lying accuser was throwing his insults at me rapid fire, and my mind was in the fetal position.

> *"You've done nothing with your life," he said. "Your God doesn't care about you. Living like this is misery, days filled with poverty and shame. Your husband is no help, and all he cares about is ministry. He married you to serve him, but he doesn't love you. You're ill-matched. If you stay here, you're a goner. You should leave. You should flee. You'd be happier somewhere else where you could afford babysitters and maintain sanity. You deserve a life where your husband takes you on dates and cares about you. You need a place where you have a successful job and an identity. You've sacrificed long enough. This train isn't going to stop. It's time for you to make your own future. Stop thinking there's a god that loves you. Quit wasting your life."*

It was the climax moment, and I knew it. I could flee, as was my custom. I could continue to suffer the mental torment, watching my light go out, or I could pick up the sword and start swinging. The enemy would either plant his flag of victory, or I would sever the grip he had on me. Only one of us could survive.

* * *

I've always been a sucker for a case of injustice. From watching a dominating kid cut in line at a playground to an innocent person falsely accused, any type of unfairness sets me off pretty quickly. I think it's mostly to do with that deep commitment to following the rules. A situation of injustice is the only type I can think of that sparks an immediate reaction within me. I'm instantly invested in the situation. My nerves can't rest until I see justice prevail.

I'm also a big chicken (I guess non-confrontational is more complimentary). After the tenth time watching the kid cut in line, I might finally let him know that cutting isn't cool, but I'd likely only mention it if his parents weren't around. If the parents were present, I'd probably take my kid to another area to play, or I'd just go home. Chances are, none of the other children playing at the park had even noticed the sly dog cutting in line, but I typically do, and changing the scenery is often a good idea.

From all the situations I've already described, whether they were entirely accurate or not, my life felt like six years of injustice after injustice. For years, the only emotion I remember feeling was rage. I was angry at God for not defending the innocent. I was angry at brothers and sisters in Christ for choosing ignorance. I was angry at my husband for not rescuing me. I was often angry at my children for always interrupting any moment of peace or restoration I tried to find. I wasn't perfect. My family wasn't perfect. But I wanted to see justice prevail. I wanted to see the deceitful fall and the humble lifted up. I wanted the Lord to rescue me from this misery.

According to psychologists, bottling up your emotions apparently isn't the best coping mechanism. But that was my default reaction. I had been burying my anger for years. I'd watch nonsensical sitcoms in the evenings to attempt to kill my brain and numb my feelings. It was effective as a Band-Aid, but I'd wake up each morning with the anger still there. By believing lies, I thought I had no one left to turn to. Everyone I loved now felt like an enemy. Typical frustrations with children left me feeling psychotic. I wasn't going to hurt them or myself, but I didn't know how to cope emotionally. I'm not a crier, I don't like complaining, and I'd rather fix an issue than address a person. My husband would come home and know something was up, but I'd continue to reply, "I'm fine."

As I dragged my feet through the valley, all the other believers seemed to be smiling. As my face revealed the agony of my toxic wounds, it was as if they had never been in a battle. Like newscasters, they didn't seem to experience the emotions of life. I know we are not to constantly wear our emotions on our sleeve, but there was something too robotic happening. I heard the implication: I was alone. No one seemed to be struggling. No one seemed to be experiencing spiritual warfare. Either they hid a ton of skeletons in their closet, or I was the only one who had traveled off course. It seemed that I had missed the Kool-Aid, or maybe I was the only one who drank it.

I knew Satan was behind much of the mental anguish, but it felt like I was drowning and had forgotten how to swim. I wanted God to pull me out, but only if he came as the God of the Bible and not this Christian-culture-influenced god who had hurt me so badly. I didn't know how to save myself. The Lord would have to come and rescue me.

So he did. He didn't convict me with bolts of lightning. He didn't hold my hand and cuddle me. He didn't give me a million dollars or a box of tissues. He didn't send missionaries to my door. He didn't press it upon me to open his Word. He knew me well enough to know those things wouldn't help me return to him, at least not in my current condition. As I mentioned in the first chapter, God sent a band. The beats of their songs allowed me to work out my anger. I felt safe to let the anger rise and then to let it go. The lyrics were raw and honest. You can interpret songs however you like, but these musicians seemed to understand seasons of spiritual warfare. They seemed to understand doubt. If I had written the lyrics myself, they couldn't have been more applicable. What was the Lord's first message to me during this time? What did I need to know that would soften my heart? *You're not alone.*

I hadn't realized how lonely I had felt during those years. This message was like a match in the darkness. "You're not alone" was life-giving. "You're not alone" could make me smile and cry at the same time. God wasn't telling me that all my emotional responses were validated, but he understood why I experienced them. At that moment, the moment God lit the match in the darkness, I didn't realize how much grace he was showing. I didn't realize how much love he had for me. I'm sure I still don't. But for a God who hates sin, I now know a little more about his unwavering faithfulness.

* * *

It's funny how we quote certain scriptures as if they pertain more than others. It's like how we talk about Satan prowling around like a lion and that we should resist him. Do you know what comes directly after those words? It's the encouragement, in my opinion. It's the comfort. 1 Peter 5:9 says, "Resist him, firm in your faith, *knowing that the same kinds of suffering are being experienced by your brotherhood throughout the world*" (ESV, emphasis mine). The devil exists, and none of us are immune to his prowling. But, you are not alone.

CHAPTER TEN

YOU HAVE NO FUTURE

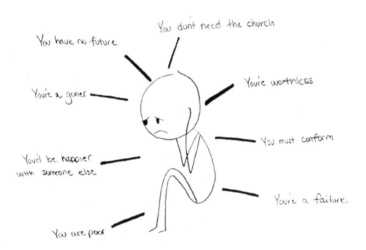

Be on your guard; stand firm in the faith; be courageous; be strong.

—1 Corinthians 16:13, NIV

It was a pleasant Thursday morning. My older children were at school, and I had dropped off my youngest at pre-school. My husband was teaching, and I didn't bother telling him where I was going. This needed to be done quickly, or I'd panic and back out. My over-thinking personality and lack of impulsiveness would send me packing. This was never something on my list of things to do in life. I didn't admire others who had chosen to do it. I'd be judged by some for going through with it, but I knew I had to commit. I knew I couldn't hesitate in the purpose that was revealed to me. If I went through with this first step, I wouldn't be able to turn back. I had to do this to fight the fear. I had to do it to fight the doubt. I wasn't going to allow the enemy any more ground than he had attempted to take. I parked downtown, walked across the street, and sat down. I heard the buzz, felt the needles, and watched the artist make the first mark of the tattoo.

A much bigger flame had ignited from that tiny match the Lord had given me a year ago. It was strange, because it wasn't like the Sunday school stories I remember. The Lord provided a match in the darkness, not for me to see him in all his glory, but for me to see my enemy. I had known truth, I had known the Lord, I had known his love, but I reached the point where half of me wanted to turn from him while the other half was terrified he'd left me. My reasoning and logic were driving me mad, and I couldn't see the forest for the trees. I grew up hearing very little about Satan. I knew he existed, but I was unfamiliar with his tactics. I didn't think I had become his victim because I wasn't a gang member, a druggie, or a gossip, and I didn't work the street corner. But why would Satan be after people who are already following him?

The match was lit, and I was nose-to-nose with the lying murderer. I couldn't see the truth for the lies. I had been entertaining the presence of Satan by considering his theories. I had allowed the lies to be embedded in my flesh. One by one, I watched the Lord remove the false accusations. Then, I cried as he mercifully healed the wounds and defused my heart of stone. I paid close attention as the lies were extracted, knowing I never wanted to expose myself to them again. Though each accusation seemed to have several barbs, I counted a total of eight lies.

So the tattoo artist continued, until I had eight tally marks on my wrist.

* * *

I've never been interested enough in school subjects to delve into an area of study. It was my writing skills that helped me survive the academic world. Even still, I'm not a wordsmith. I like a good laugh and analogies. A few years ago, a stirring began within me that seemed to be pointing to writing a book. It was an odd stirring, one as foreign as when I was told to stay at home and raise some kids. I started tinkering around with stories, but nothing seemed significant enough to sacrifice hours of a reader's life. Then one winter morning seven months ago, a purpose surfaced. I had been right about the book part—the Lord was revealing the future he had planned for me. But my purpose was to expose Satan through writing. It was time to start swinging the sword.

Like a devoted friend, the enemy hasn't neglected to check in on my progress. In the beginning, I experienced horrific dreams that haunted me as I attempted to write. Our church prayed, and the nightmares ceased. Then came the criticisms. They danced around the common theme of "who cares?" I'd write and fight thoughts such as

Who cares what you have to say? You're a nobody. You're a stranger and no one cares about a stranger's thoughts. You think you are unique, but no one thinks of you as anything special. You're spending a lot of time and money just writing a journal. Don't be too embarrassed when a few copies sit on a couple of friends' shelves. Oh, it's a sweet sentiment, little girl, just like the picture on the fridge drawn by your three-year-old.

Why do I call Satan a bully? Because I'm not supposed to use explicit language.

When the doubt would affect my productivity, I'd ask for help from friends and the church. They would pray, and the Lord would send affirmation from several different angles. But why was it difficult to resist the pettiness of these attacks? Because the accuser still uses the same tactics he did with Eve: rephrase an element of truth, twisting it to make you doubt the Lord. The truth is, I am a nobody in this world. This book is nothing but my struggle through a season of spiritual warfare. I don't have a background in writing, I haven't been to seminary, and the only published work to my name is a poem written in sixth grade about having teeth made out of candy.[1] On the second page of the application, my current publisher requested information about my platform (my presence on social media). I had a good laugh with that one. I shared a Facebook page with my husband and told two people I was writing a book. That portion of the application was largely blank upon submission.

There is no reason this book should impact others and be viewed as a success, except one: God has told me it will. I have been given freedom, but it is not just for myself. I am to share this freedom with others because I am not alone. There are many children of God who have been bullied by Satan, and the Lord's might and compassion are about to be released. I am to expose these lies because they will help crumble thousands of invisible prisons. I am to write this book, allowing God to use me as a match in the darkness—a match exposing Satan—a match breathing new strength into the army of the Lord—a match putting an even bigger target on my back, but I don't care.

I have been given purpose and a future, and Satan has tried relentlessly to persuade me otherwise. He has attempted to steal and kill my purpose while the Lord has paved my path. I know that for me to doubt writing this book is for me to doubt the Lord, his wisdom, his future for my life, and what he is able to do through whomever he asks. If exposing Satan's attempts brings freedom to another believer, every ounce of effort has been worth it. If I never hear of its impacts, I will rejoice in knowing I have been faithful to the Lord's request.

Prior to the Lord revealing the aims of our enemy, I would have succumbed to doubt and found a safe job in which I was qualified to work. I would have made my own future, too scared to trust the Lord enough to go out on a limb. Those days have passed, however. Aware of the sly moves of this seducer, I'm also more aware of the depths of God's love. He is a God who loves his children enough to follow them as they pout, wait until they have stopped running, reveal the ways they have entrapped themselves, and offer a path back to safety. I trust that even if his prompting does not result in a future the world would praise, he has my best interests in mind. Who am I to doubt his wisdom?

* * *

Many people downplay the purpose of their lives because they think their gifts can't impact the greater world. Although I understand their struggle, we are often guilty of removing God from the equation. We believe we are small and incapable of being used by the Lord to further his kingdom. But who told us we were small? Certainly not a God who would send his son as a sacrifice for us. And last I checked, God didn't always use the top qualifiers to achieve his will. The Lord used broken people. He gives strength to the humble. I believe he loves the glory they bring him as others watch them achieve the "impossible."

Want an example of a potentially downplayed purpose? There were several talented people who helped complete this book, but the encouragers are what made it happen. It was the text messages from those who had faith in me when mine wavered. It was those who prayed and reminded me that I was being thought of during this time. It may be simple for an affirming person to believe that words of affirmation are no big deal, but to those who have not heard them often, they are life-giving.

Our enemy wants us to believe that the future the Lord has for us is either insignificant, non-existent, or a foolish quest. He wants to steal the blessings that are found in being part of a body of believers who openly share the beauty of their hearts. He wants to rob us of those who give of themselves from the Lord's prompting, despite the risks. The enemy desires to use the wisdom of the world to make cowards of us. "For what does it profit a man to gain the whole world, and forfeit his soul?" (Mark 8:36). Are we willing to press into the gifts we have been given and freely use them to build each other up? Are we willing to take risks that, at face value, look like sacrifice? Do we have confidence in the Lord?

Why is Jeremiah 29:11, a random verse, so popular? Because the affirmation of the Lord's purpose for our lives is constantly attacked. We begin to believe that an ordinary looking life doesn't measure up to the purpose of one called by God. The question is, what is Satan trying to keep you from achieving by believing you have no purpose and no future? Is he keeping you from forgiving because you are gracious? Is he keeping you from pouring out joy because you are thankful? Is he keeping you from showing mercy because you are merciful? Is he keeping you from teaching, praying, or listening? Do you doubt your purpose because you think no one cares about what you have to offer? Kindly excuse yourself from Satan's presence and walk toward the future God has given you. You are needed. You are desired. Your gifts are cherished.

Bless your brothers and sisters in Christ by sharing your gifts with them. It's what you were created for. You have purpose. You have been given hope and a future.

* * *

A month before I sat in that tattoo parlor, I had a dream that I will never forget. The sky was a greenish-gray. I was walking with a friend on the outskirts of a field. The grass was shin-high, but dead. There were people in the center of the field dressing for combat and gathering supplies. They appeared stern, tired, and eager to finish their quest. Even though we were aware of their presence, we continued to walk casually by and chitchat. An extremely muscular man approached me and took hold of my hand, leading me to the group. It was as if I had been chosen by him to be part of this army. I felt terrified and humbled. My eyes drifted downward as he walked me closer to the people. His hair was buzzed, his shoulder was huge, his arm was covered in grime, and on his wrist were tally marks.

CHAPTER ELEVEN

WHERE THE CONCLUSION GOES

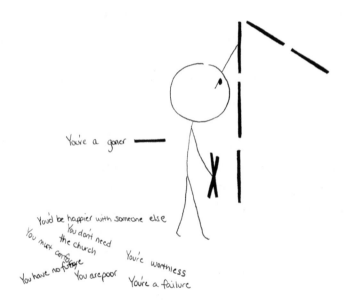

I enjoy watching magic shows when they reveal how you've been duped. It's usually a television program where they replay the trick after telling you where to focus your attention. The quickness of the movements requires talent, but the trick is often simple. I always feel like an idiot, but there's something hilarious about how easily we can be fooled. I'm certain I couldn't be a magician because I'd never stop laughing.

If you ask me, I'd say Satan is a pretty clever magician. If you noticed the titles of this book's chapters, you'd see that all the lies start with "you." Just when my focus was off, he slid in and left his lure. My own life was happening so fast that it didn't seem like the events occurred in real time. Instead of cutting out projects, stuff, or events, I tried to juggle them. There were so many balls in the air that if I shifted my focus to the Lord, I thought they would all drop. I didn't trust him to keep the items in play while I relinquished control. It was unintentional, but my actions were foolish. I knew no endeavor could succeed without him. I knew the Lord wasn't just another ball to juggle. But my cart took off without the horse, and I chased the wrong things. I was consumed with myself and trying to keep this family afloat. The focus was on me, which is a great distraction when you are being deceived.

Through some trial and error, I've learned that self-centeredness doesn't provide the return you imagined. Neither does holding on to idols. Both do provide, however, diversions for the illusionist. But like the host revealing the sleight of hand, the conclusion to our disillusionment is just as simple: Keep your eyes on the Lord.

* * *

There's a lady in our town who has succeeded in this mission. I pass by her often since she enjoys jogging seven to eight miles per day. Well, she dance-jogs seven to eight miles, but she isn't wearing ear buds. Most people drive by and assume she's a gal who's gone off her medication. She stopped by the house when my neighbor and I held a yard sale. I didn't know who she was at first when her beautiful car stopped on our street. When she got out, I guess I was caught off guard because I had assumed she didn't own a car. Our conversation started with pleasantries, but I couldn't help myself from asking more personal questions. She's in her 70s, although you could never tell. She told us several stories from her days in the Army when she jumped out of planes. She said she had volunteered for the position and paid careful attention when stuffing her parachute. Her stories were incredible, and it was obvious she was of sound mind. It was her love of Jesus that led her to dance through town. She moved to the beat of God's heart. She smiled through every word as though she were already in heaven.

I found myself wanting to love Jesus the way this woman loved him, willing to dance in the streets. Before I had the pleasure of meeting her, I'd drive by quizzically while she was running. When I see her now, I smile at the perfect confidence she has in her Parachute.

* * *

It's my hope that I haven't come across as a blame-shifter in this book. I have grieved over the condition of my heart toward the Lord. I have rejoiced in being reunited with the love of my youth, the God of the Bible who isn't filtered through human influences. But, I know how it feels to fall for deception and then have the deceiver point at you declaring, *Look what you've done!* Jesus wasn't sent to the world to condemn. He came to set the captives free (John 3:17, Luke 4:18–21). So often we run from God out of ignorance, then we pretend to hide out of shame. We are so preoccupied with the fear and terror of being found that we miss the fact that God is sitting beside us. We forget that love drives out fear (1 John 4:18). He wants to anoint our head with oil, if ever we're willing to stop burying it.

I have written this book hoping to break through to those who are in a fear-induced coma as I was. I hope I have gained your trust and that you find it worth inching back toward love. Keeping your eyes set on him, he will heal you of the lies you've been told. He can soften your heart if you're willing to trust him.

* * *

Act II

As we near the group of people, the man releases my hand and asks me to suit up. He disappears into the crowd. I follow the lead of others who are preparing. I don't know what I'm doing. I've never been in combat. I don't know why I was chosen. But without question, I'm compelled to offer whatever I have to their mission. You can see on each person's face that their quest is a noble one. No one's eyes are filled with hatred or malice. In fact, it doesn't seem like they are focused on an enemy at all. Their faces are torn with compassion. They are silent as they stuff their packs, thinking about those they are attempting to rescue. I'm not sure who has been captured, but each of these people is willing to die to see the captives freed.

I have one boot on when a man comes by and hands me a ready pack. I'm either late for this event or there is no time to waste. I slide on the other boot a bit faster. The people begin moving toward the other end of the field. I hear where we're headed. No one speaks as we wait. No one looks down. Their lack of fear helps me stay calm.

The man with the tally marks is on the edge of the chopper, grabbing arms and helping people on board. The line has moved much faster, and suddenly it's my turn. He pulls me in without making eye contact. It's as if these people think their entire mission could fail if they lose focus for an instant. I find a seat. I don't know where we're going or how long it will take us to get there. I don't know how I'll recognize who will need rescuing when we arrive. The sun is setting, and I'm wondering how difficult this task will be in the dark. A stirring begins at the end of my row. They're passing out night vision goggles. As soon as a pair hits my hands, the people begin to stand. We must have arrived. A part of me wants to hesitate, but I rise. A smaller guy, about my age, walks over, turns on my goggles, and walks away. I can see clearly now, though the world is dark. There's a moment when time seems to stand still, and then the passengers begin to disappear. I'm left standing next to the man. He pats my back two times and motions me to go. Trusting there's a parachute somewhere in this pack, I jump.

* * *

ACKNOWLEDGMENTS

My deep thanks to the encouragers, those who believe in God's ability to use the oddest of vessels. You can change the world. Thanks to my husband, the best encourager of them all, for your unwavering faith in this mission. Thanks to Steve Knox for believing in people. Thanks to Lucid Books for seeing who-knows-what in the few sentences I sent their way and having faith in the outcome. Special thanks to Megan Poling, Laurie Waller, and Sammantha Lengl for your kindness in fielding the extra questions a rookie asks.

Thanks to my fellow unicorn, Natalie Hanemann, for your time and energy spent editing this book. Thanks to Jordan Jones, Adrienne Bauer, and Jason Rowe for helping make this thing the best it can be.

My friends have many talents. Thanks to Ben Keeling and Natalie Clemmons for your amazing photography skills and the many days of breaking bread together.

Thanks to our church for allowing me to heal beside you. Thanks to Jennifer Harrell for your friendship during the darkness. Thanks to Twenty One Pilots for being the match.

LET'S DISCUSS

Chapter 1

1. Do you have a favorite family heritage story? What is it?
2. Name some tactics used in hunting. Do we know of examples in scripture where Satan or his demons use similar tactics?
3. Read Genesis 3:1–7.
4. Have you ever thought of Eve as being weak? Do you think you would have fallen for the temptation, trusting Satan that you would become like God, and risking God's warning of death?
5. Why would Eve have taken the risk?
6. It's not advisable for a believer to focus too much on spiritual warfare, to become obsessed with our enemy, nor to gloat on the power we hold over him. However, to never consider his possible interactions with our lives may be problematic. How do we achieve a healthy spiritual balance of knowing our enemy but not being consumed by it?

Chapter 2

1. What's the most ignorant thing you've been persuaded to do (that you're willing to share)?
2. When you think of asking for forgiveness of sins, do you tend to focus on acts or the heart behind the acts? Why?
3. Do you agree that your sins reflect your beliefs, disbeliefs, or doubts regarding God? Why or why not?
4. Are you in the habit of putting on the armor of God, or do these verses get lumped into your frequently-used-scripture box?
5. If we face trials in this life and have the ability to be enticed by our own sinful desires, and if we face an enemy who desires to persuade us, do we need the armor of God? If yes, why do we often go through our days without it?
6. How can we remain steadfast and diligent in putting on the armor?

Chapter 3

1. If you were to walk into a setting with a group of strangers, what would help make you feel most comfortable (walking back out is not an option)?
2. When you encounter a confrontation or even a mere inconvenience someone has caused you, are you more likely to immediately respond by taking offense or by showing grace?
3. How can the habit of taking offense be destructive in our lives?

4. How does your church appear to an outsider? Does it look like one that's full of bickering politicians or one that loves unconditionally, full of grace and forgiveness?
5. Read Hebrews 10:23–25. What are the benefits found in "not forsaking our own assembling together"?

Chapter 4

1. Do you have a hidden talent? What is it?
2. What evidence do we find in society that points to the fact that each of us, for the most part, struggle with self-worth?
3. How can we remain thankful for the gifts in our lives while not deriving our worth from them? (Example: We've been blessed with the highest promotion within the company. How does it not go to our heads?) Can you think of any scripture that may help keep our hearts in the right place in the matter?
4. What are the dangers in deriving our worth from the here and now?
5. What does your current opinion about your worth or value translate to the world about God?

Chapter 5

1. Superheroes, by definition, are different from the norm in some way. Who's your favorite superhero? Why?
2. Do you think the church embraces creativity or is afraid of it? Are there times when the church should be cautious? Can the church be cautious without removing individuals' ability to think?

3. Do you think it's possible that the spirit of the age is one of agreement, support, and service? If so, how could Satan attempt to use this to his benefit?

4. If someone your church has served were asked their opinion of God based on their interaction with the church, what would their answer include? Would they say God is full of grace but will also one day judge each of us? Would they wonder where God is between the major holidays?

5. What's your favorite way to serve the body of Christ? What's your favorite way to serve the lost (if different)?

6. What's your gift of the Spirit?

Chapter 6

1. What was your first legit job (i.e., they took out taxes)? Did you love it or hate it?

2. How do you respond when you find yourself unprepared for a task?

3. When you began following Jesus, would you have walked away grieving had Jesus asked you to sell everything you owned and give it to the poor? Would you grieve if he asked it of you now?

4. Do we have a certain standard of life we expect God to maintain for us? Is that standard biblical (show proof in scripture)?

5. How could Satan use comfort and wealth to lead us astray?

Chapter 7

1. If you possessed the skills to succeed at any job, which job would you choose? Why?
2. Is there a possibility God will hold us accountable for the finances he has given us?
3. Do we see resources as given by God and under our care so that we are attempting to manage them in a way that brings him glory? Or do we see them as gifts from God and then we turn away, clenching our fists?
4. How do we live life serving one master—God—and not money?

Chapter 8

1. What's the worst date you've been on?
2. Describe some of the examples of marriage you encountered growing up.
3. Do we see the differences in our spouse as a pro or a con to the relationship? How can we appreciate our differences but also recognize when iron should sharpen iron?
4. Are you receptive to your spouse's sharpening? Do you react out of offense or see the comment as made out of love and for the good of the team?
5. Do you make decisions (how to spend your time, money, and mind power) based on what's best for the team (your family)? Does this come naturally?
6. How should our marriages reflect Christ and the church?

Chapter 9

1. How do you cope with stress?
2. Does our vulnerability level within the body of Christ correlate with how isolated people may feel during a trial? Is there a way to be vulnerable without constantly airing our dirty laundry?
3. How can feeling alone add to the stress of a trial? How is knowing you are not alone empowering?
4. Are we aware enough to recognize when a brother or sister in Christ is struggling? Are we too self-absorbed to pause and walk beside them?

Chapter 10

1. Have you ever reached a climax point in your faith? What was it?
2. Do you typically only consider Satan being active in the lives of those blatantly full of sin? Is this perspective biblical? How can it be dangerous?
3. Do we take the potential purposes for our lives and subconsciously establish a hierarchy of which are most honorable (according to our standards)? How could this be dangerous?
4. Why do you think we hear or read the statement in Jeremiah 29:11 so often?
5. Can you think of an area or gift that Satan may be trying to downplay in your life, attempting to persuade you to think the gift or act isn't that big of a deal?

Chapter 11

1. What's the most fascinating magic trick you remember seeing?
2. If keeping our eyes focused on the Lord can prevent us from being deceived, how can we remained focused in a world full of distractions? Is it important to do so?
3. Has this story revealed any invisible walls of lies in your life? Share if you'd like.
4. What's your Act II?

NOTES

Chapter 1

1. The Myers & Briggs Foundation, "How Frequent Is My Type," accessed November 3, 2017, http://www.myersbriggs.org/my-mbti-personality-type/my-mbti-results/how-frequent-is-my-type.htm.

2. The devil holding a pitchfork has no biblical roots. Since the imagery of a unicorn is already ludicrous, I decided the use of a pitchfork seemed just as likely.

3. The subject of this book revolves around spiritual warfare, but it is not my intention to make warfare the focus of our lives. It is my intention to help others rejoice even more in their salvation through Christ by dislodging any lies they may have unintentionally entertained along the way.

Chapter 2

1. Wayne Grudem, *Systematic Theology* (Grand Rapids, MI: Zondervan, 1994), 412.

2. Ibid., 415.

3. This concept is widely held by most scholars. One explanation is found in this source. John MacArthur, *The MacArthur Study Bible* (Nashville, TN: Thomas Nelson, 1997), 1342.

Chapter 3

1. Grudem, 425.

2. John Bevere, *The Bait of Satan: Living Free from the Deadly Trap of* Offense (Lake Mary, FL: Charisma House, 1994), 40.

3. Ibid., 39.

4. Ibid., 7.

5. Ibid., 6.

Chapter 4

1. Technically, this opinion is not held unanimously. Of the Batman films created during my lifetime, I was a much bigger fan of seeing him impersonate Doc Holliday.

Chapter 5

1. "INTJ Personality ('The Architect')," 16 Personalities, accessed November 3, 2017, https://www.16personalities.com/intj-personality.

2. "Disciplined," Dictionary.com, accessed November 3, 2017, http://www.dictionary.com/browse/disciplined?s=t.

3. "Conformity," Dictionary.com, accessed November 3, 2017, http://www.dictionary.com/browse/conformity?s=t.

4. John MacArthur, *The MacArthur Study Bible* (Nashville, TN: Thomas Nelson, 1997), 1716.

5. Ibid.

6. A.W. Tozer, *The Knowledge of the Holy* (New York: HarperOne, 1961), 1.

Chapter 6

1. This is my opinion. I prefer a lightweight log with a perfect grey color. Seasoned firewood has varying definitions.

2. John Piper, "Christ in Combat: Defense by the Spirit," Last modified March 18, 1984, Desiring God, http://www.desiringgod.org/messages/christ-in-combat-defense-by-the-spirit.

Chapter 10

1. "Sweet-tooth"

   Do you know what I think would be nice and dandy?
   Having teeth made out of candy.

   You could have whatever flavor you like,
   You could eat them morning, noon, and night.

   You could eat them and eat them every day,
   You'd never have to worry about tooth decay.

   Shall you ever break one of them,
   You can always replace it with an M&M.

   Dentist will no longer exist,
   Only Willy Wonka and the Hershey chocolate kiss.

   No more brushing, rinsing, flossing, or pulling,
   But hey, it's a dream so who am I fooling?

CPSIA information can be obtained
at www.ICGtesting.com
Printed in the USA
BVHW06s2352230418
514135BV00020B/420/P